CAREERS AND DISABILITIES:
A Career Education Approach

**David C. Gardner
and
Sue Allen Warren**

CAREERS AND DISABILITIES:
A Career Education Approach

David C. Gardner
and
Sue Allen Warren

GREYLOCK PUBLISHERS
13 Spring Street, Stamford, CT 06901

Printed in the United States of America.
Library of Congress Catalog Card Number: 78-62312.
ISBN: 0-89223-020-7 (hard cover).

Acknowledgements

It is always impossible for writers to acknowledge, or even remember, all the individuals who have indirectly contributed to a final product. We are indebted to former teachers, colleagues, our students and our critics. We take final responsibility for the content of this book, but we wish to thank all those who have influenced our thinking.

We want to express particular gratitude to a few persons who have directly contributed to this effort.

Paula Lyn Gardner has been a supporter, friend, and tactful critic for us both. She read the manuscript and helped to provide the classroom and university teacher perspective. Furthermore, she has been a patient and inspiring wife to a husband who spent time on this book while she assumed more than her share of the responsibility for Joshua.

The never-failing confidence and reassurance of Arthur Allen Little has encouraged his mother to keep writing, even when she was unsure that the manuscript would or could be finished.

The typist for this manuscript, Pamela Wheeler, has tolerated difficult time schedules and deciphered even more difficult writing and typing.

Finally, our parents inspired us by their examples with the importance of giving all human beings an opportunity to have meaningful work and leisure activites and taught us that contributing to society is a basic human right.

D.C.G.
S.A.W.
Boston, Massachusetts

Contents

Foreword

Finally! Recommendations for narrowing the gap between what is being taught to handicapped persons and what they need to know to make an appropriate life adjustment is presented in a practical and succint manner by Gardner and Warren in their book *Careers and Disabilities: A Career Education Approach.*

The need for an interdisciplinary text in the fields of special education and career education has been clear for several years. This authoritative text is a first...and does its job in a helpful and practical way.

The development of curricula that reflect the needs of society could offer great promise for persons that are different—especially since these differences often lie at the root of their handicaps.

The loss or absence of a limb, the dysfunction of sensory system, and/or low cognitive ability may contribute a share in making an individual handicapped, but these are not the only differences that could account for handicapping individuals. Other factors—such as inadequate or insufficient opportunities to learn—can be equally impeding. Differences in human behavior must not be considered synonymous with handicaps. The question remaining then, should be what makes a particular difference in a particular person handicapping?

It is understood that disabilities among humans may indeed interfere with their ability to learn, to get a job, and to make a normal life adjustment, but such differences are not the only or necessarily the major factors. Our society is faced with exciting technological advances; the vast movement to urbanization from rural/agricultural communities has increased our awareness for the need for differentiated educational programming. Likewise, our evolving philosophy of "education for all" has heightened our sensitivity so much that programs tailored to individualized learners cannot any longer be regarded as luxuries for a small elite group such as the wealthy or the exceptionally bright. On the contrary, individually tailored programs must be recognized as a necessity for a very large number of our country's youth if we are truly serious about our goal to foster generations of independent, contributing and responsible citizens.

The authors point out that scores, numbers, ratings, percentiles, etc., obtained from the use of assessment tools must be considered as information from which to plan the future, but not in isolation or exclusion of other important data. The *misuse* of such information could lead to additional (and unnecessary) difficulties for persons with disabilities. On the other hand, the proper use of assessment data in combination with other information could do much to help obviate individual differences from becoming/remaining handicapping conditions.

The complexity and variability among human beings makes it impossible (and improbable) that certain principles of learning which have emerged could become "the" way for teachers to teach. This has led some educators to refrain from using such established precepts and to teach, so to speak, "from the heart." The authors caution that to pay no attention to recognized principles of learning results in a predictable decrease in teaching efficiency. The implications such a decrease would have on the learning, especially for the handicapped person, are too obvious to elaborate.

Human behavior is more learned than instinctive. The authors urge persons engaged in helping others with handicaps to develop not only the processes for distinguishing crucial areas in which effective interventions can be made, but of teaching strategies that are based on learning theories. The utilization of such processes and strategies, especially those that are related to the world of work are necessary and should be encouraged. By doing so, a predictable result may be the increase in the quality and the quantity of the work performed by handicapped persons.

One's review of a school planned program, i.e., its curriculum, should provide answers to the question "for what are students being prepared?" In other words, that which goes on in school should be viewed as the identified means for attaining an identified end. It has always been curious to this writer, then, that so many curricula prepared for "special" education programs so closely resemble curricula developed for non-handicapped learners, with the major difference being the slower pace. The important question "How realistic or practical is what is being planned (or implemented) for the learners?" must be answered if one is to optimize the chances for learners with handicaps to achieve their optimal career development. Factors such as an individual's interest and employment potential, for example, must be taken into account early enough (and continued consistently) in the educational processes so as to be maximally effective.

Achieving a meaningful place in society is clearly related to the degree to which one can earn a living, which is related, of course, to how independent one is (or can become). During the past several years an increasing emphasis on education for all has emerged in our society. It is noteworthy, too, to recognize that with increasing regularity this philosophy has indeed been extended to handicapped learners. A major difference, though, may be that for such pupils the educational setting need less often be confined to in-school experiences. Comprehensive career education must not only begin very early in life but be accessible to handicapped persons in a variety of physical locations.

A major challenge facing educators of handicapped persons is to reduce the prevailing differences between what is being taught and what is needed to achieve a high degree of life adjustment.

Careers and Disabilities: A Career Education Approach offers many practical suggestions and provides much useful information from which to narrow this existing gap. This publication will undoubtedly be of great value to many professional persons.

Albert J. Berkowitz
Executive Director
American Association on Mental Deficiency
Washington, D.C.
1978

Chapter I

Career Education: Focus on the Handicapped

Benjamin, the oldest son of an upper middle class family, recently graduated from a college preparatory program in a public high school, with honors. During the spring following graduation, Ben refused to apply for college as planned. He even refused to consider looking for employment by August following graduation. From discussion with his parents, it soon became obvious that Ben had a limited knowledge of the myriad career possibilities open to him. Also, Ben had failed to acquire appropriate attitudes toward work and was "turned off by the whole job scene." As far as Ben was concerned, according to his parents, school and work were both "irrelevant."

This case is typical of the many problems confronting Americans today as they attempt to deal with *rapidly changing technology, shifting labor markets, and conflicting values about work and society.*

Take the case of Mary, for instance. Mary is a very unhappy college senior enrolled in a private university and although she has looked, she can't find a job. Mary cannot understand why no one seems interested in her when she will very shortly receive a very expensive college degree in foreign languages. When it was explained to her that the job market for foreign language graduates is limited, and, at the minimum requires that one be fluent in several languages, Mary complained that no one had told her all this beforehand. Mary says that she has always believed that a college degree would lead to a good job. Mary has learned now that a *college degree is no longer a ticket to a good job.* She has also learned that her college program has failed to provide her with readily marketable skills for employment.

Similarly, Janice, who has recently earned a doctorate in medieval history from a midwestern university, is faced with employment problems. Janice does not know how to go about looking for a job and has never written a resume. Unfortunately, Janice does not want to work in the field in which she recently earned her degree. "Besides," she murmurs, "there are no jobs." She now feels that her only salvation is to get a practical degree like a Master of Business Administration or "something like that." She has often thought that she might like to be an office manager but has not acquired the appropriate skills. Janice believes that a woman who can type and file is destined never to become more than a secretary.

These stories illustrate the many real life crises facing thousands of Americans, young and old, across the country today. These are case studies of persons *who are not handicapped.* These kinds of problems, of career development and work adjustment, *are compounded for workers and students who are handicapped.* Persons with special needs usually work side by side with non-handicapped persons in a highly competitive, work-oriented, technological society.

Today, handicapped persons must compete in a labor market which, according to the U.S. Department of Health, Education and Welfare (HEW), has the highest youth unemployment rate in the world. HEW figures indicate that approximately 2.5 million young Americans enter the labor market each year without marketable skills.

The competition for jobs is keen in all sectors of the labor market. HEW predicts that by 1980 there will be 9.6 million jobs for a 9.8 million college graduates. For handicapped persons, the labor market is increasingly competitive with many of the traditional unskilled jobs normally associated with employment for some handicapped populations disappearing. In 1972, for instance, one expert predicted that only 21% of handicapped persons leaving school will be fully employed or go on to college; 40% will be underemployed; 25% will be unemployed; 10% will work in sheltered programs or stay home; and 3% will be totally dependent. These estimates were made before the current recession. A more recent estimate suggests that nearly 80% of American workers (those with jobs), handicapped and non-handicapped, are either *underemployed* or *misemployed.*

These distressing statistics suggest a malfunctioning of our educational delivery system as it relates to career development. Many of the economic-sociological-psychological problems of today have been directly attributed to our educational system which seems to have failed to provide for the work dimensions of our culture. One recently emerging response to the failures of our educational process is called "career education." Career education offers alternatives to the present curricula, which has too long failed to focus on the importance of work preparation and career development to total human development. It has failed to provide relevant training for a great majority of our youth, especially disabled individuals.

A Reform Movement

Career education is a reform movement in American education (Marland, 1974), a proposal for reform which offers "...a comprehensive and long-range solution to many of America's social problems." (Gardner, 1973, p. 74). According to Kenneth Hoyt, Director of the Office of Career Education, United States Office of Education (USOE), it seeks to correct some of the many failures of American education. As you read the USOE list of prime criticisms below, you may see how the problems of Janice, Mary and Ben are related to some of these items. You will think of examples from your experiences with friends, relatives, or acquaintances, whose work dissatisfactions also relate to one or more of these criticisms.

USOE List of Prime Criticisms of Education:

1. Too many persons leaving our educational system are deficient in the basic academic skills required for adaptability in today's rapidly changing society.
2. Too many students fail to see meaningful relationships between what they are being asked to learn in school and what they will do when they leave the educational system. This is true of both those who remain to graduate and those who drop out of the educational system.
3. American education, as currently structured, best meets the educational needs of that minority of persons who will some day become college graduates. It fails to place equal emphasis on meeting the educational needs of that vast majority of students who will never be college graduates.
4. American education has not kept pace with the rapidity of change in the postindustrial occupational society. As a result, when worker qualifications are compared with job requirements, we find that over-educated and under-educated workers are present in large numbers. Both the boredom of the over-educated worker and the frustration of the under-educated worker have contributed to growing worker alienation in the total occupational society.
5. Too many persons leave our educational system at both the secondary and collegiate levels unequipped with the vocational skills, the self-understanding and career decision-making skills, or the work attitudes that are essential for making a successful transition from school to work.
6. The growing need for and presence of women in the work force has not been reflected adequately in either the educational or the career options typically pictured for girls enrolled in our educational system.
7. The growing needs for continuing and recurrent education of adults are not being met adequately by our current systems of public education.

8. Insufficient attention has been given to learning opportunities which exist outside the structure of formal education and are increasingly needed by both youth and adults in our society.
9. The general public, including parents and the business-industry-labor community, has not been given an adequate role in the formulation of educational policy.
10. American education, as currently structured, does not adequately meet the needs of minority or economically disadvantaged persons in our society.
11. Post high school education has given insufficient emphasis to educational programs at the sub-baccalaureate degree level (Hoyt, 1975, p. 1-2).

Career education can be viewed as a response to these criticisms of American education. While not the only possible response, career education is a viable one.

An Unprecedented Momentum

Career education is a reform movement which is attracting the interest of many educators, as well as community, business, industrial and labor leaders. Since 1971, when Sidney Marland, Jr. (then U.S. Commissioner of Education), announced career education as a priority area of the USOE, the efforts of the many supporters of the movement culminated in the establishment of an Office of Career Education in Washington, Congressional legislation on career education (1974), the publication of a policy paper on career education by the USOE (Hoyt, 1975), and the founding of the National Association for Career Education by a group of career education practitioners in 1974 (Gardner and Smith, 1975).

In the context of our work-oriented culture, the basic appeal of career education's philosophy, conceptual framework, and its promise, may at least partially explain its remarkable acceptance by laymen and professionals alike.

Definition of Career Education

Career education has been defined in varying ways by many persons in the field. Marland (1974) devotes an entire chapter in his new book to defining career education. The following definition, which appears in both editions of a best selling career education book authored by Kenneth Hoyt, R. Evans, E. Mackin and G. Mangum (1972, 1974) is probably the most quoted definition:

> Career education is the total effort of public education and the community to help all individuals become familiar with the values of a work-oriented society, to integrate these values into their personal value systems, and to implement these values in their lives in such a way that work becomes possible, meaningful, and satisfying to each individual (Hoyt, *et al*, 1974, p. 15).

In the recently published U.S. Office of Education (USOE) policy paper on career education, Hoyt (1975) defines career education as

...the totality of experiences through which one learns about and prepares to engage in work as part of her or his way of living (p. 4).

The USOE definition is further clarified by defining such key words as "career," "education," and "work."

"Work" is defined as

...conscious effort, other than that involved in activities whose primary purpose is either coping or relaxation, aimed at producing benefits for oneself and/or for oneself and others (p. 3).

A "career" is seen as the "...totality of work one does in his or her lifetime," and "education" as the "...totality of experiences through which one learns" (p. 3).

In interpreting these and other definitions related to career education, there are certain concepts upon which most definers agree. The first is that career education should be viewed as a *developmental* approach in its process and practice and that it is *applicable to persons of all ages,* from early childhood through adult years. Another is that career education should be multi-institutional; sharing the responsibility for career education implementation are the family, school, community, business, labor and industry.

Career education is viewed by most practitioners as an *integrating* or *"fusion"* medium and not as an add-on item in the curriculum. They explain that career education is not synonymous with vocational education or with counseling. Yet both vocational guidance and vocational education are considered by all career educators as important components in any career education model.

Most career educators would support the notion that a fundamental principle in career education is that the totality of all educational experiences, including instruction, guidance and curricula, should focus on helping each individual prepare for an *independent* life, a life of personal self-actualization and dignity in the world of work. The goal of independent functioning, in the community, as a contributing working member of society, is for all persons, including the handicapped.

Marland (1974) pointed out that in the final analysis, it is the individual, the teacher, the school administrator, the school system, the community, *those practicing career education,* who will do the defining.

Basic Principles of Career Education

The following principles underlie the programmatic approaches of career education practitioners. These are paraphrased from a 1972 USOE publication entitled *Career Education Handbook for Implementation* (p. 7-8).

1. Since a key objective of all education should be preparation for successful working careers, then,
   a. every teacher in every course will emphasize, where appropriate, the relationship between subject matter and its possible contribution to a successful working career.
   b. teachers and the school system will adopt hands-on occupationally oriented experiences as methods for teaching

academic subjects as well as for motivating students to learn abstract content.

2. Since career preparation involves the acquisition of appropriate work attitudes and human relations skills, familiarity with the world of work and alternate career choices, and the mastery of actual job skills, the classroom is viewed as only one of many learning environments in career education. Learning should also take place in the community, the home, and on the job.

3. Since career education is seen as developmental in nature, a "cradle to the grave approach," it must provide for (1) early childhood career education, (2) career education during the regular school years, (3) open entry/exit programming for youth and adults who wish to acquire experience and then re-enter the system at any time for further education and job skill upgrading. The open entry/exit principle includes refurbishing adult workers for productive use of leisure time and retirement years.

4. Another important principle places the responsibility on the schools to provide continuing placement, counseling and career preparation-retraining services for graduates and dropouts alike until each has built a firm foundation for her or his career.

These and other principles and practices of career education are based in part on research findings, and in part on professional judgments (clinical hunches) and observations. They have been restated as twenty-five testable hypotheses under the heading "Programmatic Assumptions of Career Education" in the USOE policy paper on career education (Hoyt, 1975, p. 5).

Some examples:

1. If students can see relationships between what they are being asked to learn in school and the world of work, they will be motivated to learn more in school.

6. Work values, as part of one's personal value system, are developed to a significant degree during the elementary school years and are modifiable during those years.

12. The same general strategies utilized in reducing worker alienation in industry can be used to reduce worker alienation among pupils and teachers in the classroom.

20. Relationships between education and work can be made more meaningful through infusion into subject matter than if taught as a separate body of knowledge (Hoyt, 1975, pp. 5-7).

Implications for Change

The testing of the USOE's twenty-five programmatic assumptions of career education through the implementation and evaluation of career education programs is to some extent underway in a growing number of communities across the country. For the programmatic assumptions of career education to be fully tested some basic changes in our educational system must occur. Dr. Hoyt has outlined some of the major changes called for in an essay entitled "Career education: myth or magic."

Some examples:

(1) The elimination of the concept, "school dropout" by establishing an open-entry/exit system of education in the U.S.A. (2) The increased use of the project approach to instruction. This approach emphasizes individualization of instruction and small class size. (3) The development of a new system for granting educational credit to students for tasks performed outside schools under the supervision of non-certified teachers. (4) The establishment of comprehensive counseling, placement, career guidance, and follow-up services for all youth and adults whether enrolled in school or not. (5) The adoption of performance evaluation as the primary method for measuring educational outcomes. (6) The use of educational facilities on a 12-month basis for increased efficiency in training youth and adults. Such an approach would allow for flexible scheduling of programs and permit teachers to acquire experience outside the field of education (see Hoyt, 1973, p. 29-30).

Career Education In Practice

Career education "models" are being developed at both state and local levels with varying degrees of definition (and funding) across the country. The federal government has established four models and is currently spending millions of dollars on research and development efforts in career education, including special projects for handicapped persons.

Four Models

The most widely discussed model funded by the USOE is the School-Based Comprehensive Career Education model. The school-based model provides career education for students in a K-Life educational system. This model will be described in more detail in the section below.

Other models funded by USOE are (1) the Experience-Based model, (2) the Home/Community-Based model, (3) the Rural-Residential model.

The Experience Based Model (EBCE)

At first labeled the Employer-Based model, EBCE offers an alternative system of secondary education to youths from 13 to 18 years old. According to an undated brochure entitled "The community is the teacher" published by the National Institute of Education (NIE), students in Philadelphia, Pennsylvania; Charleston, West Virginia; Oakland, California; and Tigard, Oregon, have been "exchanging ideas with and learning from adults in the everyday world." (p. 2). On page 4 of the undated NIE brochure, the EBCE model is further characterized as pulling together the

...many innovations transforming American education today under various names—schools without walls, action learning, individually prescribed instruction, competency-based certification, survival education.

In a 1975 NIE booklet bearing the same title as the undated brochure, the EBCE model is distinguished from traditional work/study programs on the basis that the program does not emphasize vocational skills per se, that EBCE is unpaid experience, that EBCE includes career exploration and employer-site rotation procedures, that EBCE uses experiential education for conveying learning in academic areas, that EBCE allows a greater student role in shaping a personalized educational plan and, lastly, that EBCE is not targeted to dropouts, disadvantaged, or other specific populations (p. 3).

The Home-Community Based Model

The Home/Community based model was originally conceptualized to be a system for providing educational services to the home. In operation in Providence, Rhode Island, since October, 1972 under the auspices of the Educational Development Corporation, Newton, Massachusetts, this NIE sponsored project has, in fact, focused on providing career counseling services by telephone for adults using a paraprofessional system. The project has also operated a Resource Center which contains career-related materials for and about adults. The project has also published five manuals, annotated bibliographies, and a film. The home/community based model

> ...has served over 5,000 men and women, aged 16 to 70, with different employment histories, education, economic levels and career aspirations. Because the target group has been defined as home-based...most of the project's clients have been women. (EDC, 1975, p. 3.)

Rural Residential Model

This model is being developed by the Mountain-Plains Education and Economic Development Program, Inc. It focuses on providing services for chronically underemployed, multi-problem rural families. It offers training, remedial education, guidance for children, career counseling and job placement for entire families with the goal of making the family unit economically viable.

Heads of households are expected to participate a minimum of 40 hours per week in the program; spouses may participate 20-40 hours per week. Program areas include home management, health education, counseling, career guidance, foundation education and occupational preparation in carpentry, plumbing, electrical, air conditioning, lodging and food services, transportation, office education, marketing and distribution.

The School-Based Comprehensive Career Education Model (CCEM)

The central theme of this U.S. Office of Education (USOE) model can best be described as an attempt to reform the curriculum of the established public school system. The prime contractor for the CCEM is the Center for Vocational and Technical Education at Ohio State University. The Center has selected six local school districts as sites for field testing and development of career education materials: Mesa, Arizona;

Pontiac, Michigan; Hackensack, New Jersey; Jefferson County, Colorado; Los Angeles, California and Atlanta, Georgia.

In addition to these federally-funded models, a number of states and many local school systems have developed (or are developing) their own models of career education. The USOE has maintained that the basic form of Career Education will have to be developed at the local and state levels. There is little doubt, however, that results of these multi-million dollar efforts will profoundly affect future developmental efforts.

Practitioners have generally utilized a four or five stage model with some stages overlapping one another. Even a cursory review of texts in the field of career education would indicate that a very popular mode is the pyramid-like model (inverted or upright). Frequently illustrated models appear to be the "USOE Inverted Pyramid" and "The Oregon Way." Figure I-1 is illustrative of most models.

FIGURE I-1

Illustrative Stages of
School-based Models

STAGE I

Usually referred to as the Career Awareness Stage. Some models grade K-4, K-5, or K-6. Concerned with self-awareness of students. No attempt to "train." The Oregon Model is K-6. In this model, students are expected to develop awareness of many careers available, awareness of self in relation to careers, respect and appreciation for all workers in all fields, and to make tentative choices of career clusters to explore in mid-school years. General approach has been to integrate career awareness into the existing curriculum, (e.g. reading, science, math, and social studies). Other strategies include examining the community's world of work through guest speakers and field trips.

STAGE II

Commonly referred to as the Career Exploration Stage. Begins around grades 5 or 6 and extends into the middle school or junior high school. Students begin to explore several of the 15 USOE occupational clusters. Oregon model extends from grades 7-10. Students' objectives include exploration of key occupational areas, assessment of career interests and abilities, development of awareness of relevent decision-making factors, gaining experience in meaningful decision making, development of tentative occupational plans; students arrive at tentative career choice. Students explore the world of work and receive "hands-on" experiences. Also can involve field trips, career resource centers, career laboratories (simulations), paid and unpaid work experience, etc.

STAGE III

Generally called the Career Preparation Stage. Approximately grades 9-12. Major goal is for students to develop either entry-level job skills or be prepared for advanced occupational training. Ideal model eliminates college preparatory, vocational, and general tracks. The Oregon Model encompasses grades 11-12. Oregon students are expected to acquire entry-level skills or be prepared for advanced vocational training, develop appropriate job attitudes, and obtain work experience. An often cited example of an outstanding secondary program at this stage is the Skyline Development Center in Dallas, Texas.

STAGE IV

Sometimes called the Career Specialization Stage. Portions of this stage are sometimes combined with portions of Stage III. Many models also include adult and continuing education (a possible Stage V) in this stage. The concentration here is on advanced career preparation above the high school level. Includes apprenticeships, associate degree programs, vocational certificate programs, university bachelors and advanced degree programs, etc. One concept is that this stage can take place at any age and may involve alternate periods of work and study. In the Oregon Model the emphasis is on developing specific occupational preparation and knowledge in a special job area; provisions for forming meaningful employer-employee relationships and learning skills for retraining and upgrading.

The Cluster Concept

One important challenge in implementing curriculum reform in the career education school-based model is the basic problem of how to classify the more than 20,000 jobs listed in the *Dictionary of Occupational Titles* and the Department of Labor catalog. The most reasonable solution seems to be to group jobs into related, broad clusters which can form the framework around which curriculum and instructional activities can function.

While there are a number of cluster schemes, the most widely accepted system among career educators is the 15 cluster system developed by the U.S. Office of Education (USOE). Under each cluster, in the USOE scheme, all types of jobs are included from entry level jobs through technical, skilled and professional level positions. The USOE clusters are:

Agri-Business and Natural Resource Occupations
Business and Office Occupations
Communication and Media Occupations
Construction Occupations
Consumer and Homemaking Occupations
Environmental Control Occupations
Fine Arts and Humanities Occupations
Health Occupations
Hospitality and Recreation Occupations
Manufacturing Occupations
Marine Science Occupations
Marketing and Distribution Occupations
Personal Service Occupations
Public Service Occupations
Transportation Occupations

Following the multi-stage school-based model, the school system can use the cluster approach as a framework for orienting students to careers and as a focal point for instructional and curriculum development activities. In the elementary grades, students study all clusters. In middle or junior high school, students usually choose five or six clusters to explore. Early in high school, a student may deal with one or two areas, and by the last two years in high school, concentrate on career preparation in one cluster.

The USOE has undertaken major curricular development in all fifteen clusters. These curricula are being designed to be integrated in appropriate academic areas and will soon be available. They will cover related academic areas from kindergarden through grade twelve.

Making It Work: Examples:

Remember Ben? His sister, Louise, is in a second grade classroom where the teacher tries to make all appropriate activities relate to the world of work. Louise's teacher has attended several workshops on career education and receives consultation from the elementary career education coordinator. Nearly half of the parents in Louise's class have participated in various career education activities.

Presently, the class is completing a unit on the Postal Service. Among the many activities completed and/or planned are field trips to small post office branches in preparation for a trip to the main post office, a lesson on the history of the postal service, interviews with their own mailmen, viewing films and filmstrips on various postal service occupations, role playing different postal service occupations, and so forth.

Louise and her classmates follow the same curriculum content as previous elementary classes: language arts, social studies, science, arithmetic, art and music. However, correlating activities in each content area are integrated with the unit. For instance, students read stories related to post office workers and are making a picture dictionary of new words introduced in the unit (language arts). They also have used a scale to practice weighing packages of different weights and computed the costs for mailing each package (arithmetic).

Mary's brother, Bill, is a senior in a regional comprehensive high school. Bill has chosen automotive technology as his area of career concentration and preparation. Bill has worked two summers in a service station and continues to work several evenings and Saturdays. He receives academic credit for this experience and is supervised by a placement coordinator. During the school year, he spends alternate weeks in an automotive technology shop and in academic class rooms under the supervision of an interdisciplinary team of teachers. Each teacher attempts to individualize classroom activities and assignments to relate to Bill's interest in the automotive field. Bill's boss has already promised him a full-time job upon graduation. Bill plans to take management courses at a community college at night while he works full-time. His long-range goal is to own his own service station.

The Status of the Handicapped in Career Education

The goals of the career education movement apply to the handicapped as well as non-handicapped persons. The majority of the mildly retarded, learning disabled and other mildly handicapped children should benefit from the implementation of career education programming similar to that used for "normal" children. The current trend towards the integration or mainstreaming of exceptional children into regular classrooms is designed to ensure their participation in career education programs in schools where career education has been adopted. In this context, the future of career education for the handicapped is tied to the future of the general career education movement.

On the other hand, many of the goals and constructs of the career education movement have been a part of the special education curricula for decades, especially for the mentally retarded at the secondary level. The present USOE emphasis on career-related objectives is likely to reinforce the continued presence of occupationally-oriented materials and strategies in the special education curricula.

Moreover, the United States Office of Career Education has recognized that it must provide *special programs* and *services* for persons whose handicapping condition may affect their career development and employment. Provisions in the career education legislation recently passed by Congress (1974) has provided funds for career education for "special needs" programs for disabled students. The United States Office of Education has funded a number of projects (e.g. Project PRICE, University of Missouri-Columbia) and results of such projects will be forthcoming. In addition, the Vocational Education Act of 1963, with subsequent amendments (1968, 1972) continues to provide funds for research and curriculum development in the vocational education of handicapped persons (e.g. Project VITA, Boston University). Faculty at several universities have developed teacher training programs for meeting the career education needs of handicapped persons (Gardner & Warren, in press). Such pre-service and graduate programs will ensure that many of the objectives of career education will find their way into the curricula for handicapped persons as these newly trained personnel enter the system. Moreover, these teachers of the handicapped should affect the personnel already in the system. At the minimum, the career education objectives already in the special education curricula will be emphasized by these new teachers.

At the adult level, the Comprehensive Employment and Training Act (CETA) and the Vocational Rehabilitation Act (1973) provide for growth in cooperative employment and training services for handicapped persons. Increasing efforts to offer career development programs for persons with special needs and to provide higher quality and greater options in vocational training programs for handicapped individuals seems assured, at least through this decade.

In summary, the career education movement will increase efforts for the handicapped by special educators (1) to eliminate the artificial distinction between academic education and education for vocational purposes in special education curricula, (2) to base curriculum content of schools on the needs of the individual handicapped person to function in society, (3) to emphasize the relationship between schools and society as a whole, including an extension of the educational process beyond the classroom into the world of work and the community, and (4) to increase the quality and quantity of guidance, counseling, career development and career placement services for handicapped persons. The purpose is to ensure that such persons develop appropriate work attitudes, values, decision-making skills, vocational skills and knowledge for *successful community living.*

FIGURE I-2

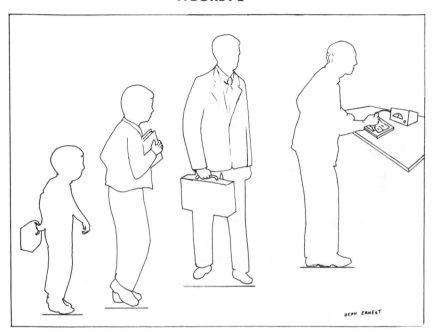

Plan of the Book

This text introduces the major concepts of the career education movement and its implications for programming for handicapped persons (Chapter I). The book also provides an overview of disabilities (Chapter II) and reviews and discusses the many barriers to employment of handicapped persons (Chapter III). It also discusses problems and techniques of vocational assessment (Chapter IV).

Chapters V, VI and VII discuss the special implications of learning theory and personality theory, illustrating from recent research, for training special needs students for the world of work.

Finally, using examples from recent studies and current programs, the last chapter focuses on "getting started." This chapter outlines how schools can find the answers to such questions as "How do we get started?" and "Where do we initiate curriculum changes?"

It is the intent of this text to deal with selected, special problem areas in career education for the handicapped. It does not detail either specific curriculum objectives or specific teaching strategies as they relate to the career education curriculum infusion process. The integration of academic and occupational curricula has been part of special education programs for decades (e.g. DeProspo & Hungerford, 1946; Hungerford, 1940). Moreover, a great many of the existing career education curriculum guides, materials and professional references for use in the public schools for normal children are easily accessible to interested special educators and readily adaptable to special programs for handicapped persons.

REFERENCES

Career counselling for adults: an overview of the home and community-based career education project. Newton, Massachusetts: Educational Development Center, Inc., U.S. Government Printing Office, 1975.

Career education: a handbook for implementation. Maryland State Board of Education, Washington, D.C.: U.S. Government Printing Office, 1972.

The community is the teacher. Washington, D.C.: National Institute of Education, U.S. Department of Health, Education and Welfare, 1975.

DeProspo, C. and Hungerford, R. A complete social program for the mentally retarded. *American Journal of Mental Deficiency,* 1946, *51,* 115-122.

Gardner, D. C. Career education in our town? *College Student Journal,* 1973, *7* (3), 73-77.

Gardner, D. C. and Smith, K. E. The National Association of Career Education. *Illinois Career Education Journal,* July, 1975.

Gardner, D.C. and Warren, S.A. A Graduate dual specialization in career education and special education. *Journal for Special Educators of the Mentally Retarded* (in press).

Hoyt, K. B. Career education: myth or magic? *NASSP Bulletin,* March, 1973, *57,* (371), 22-30.

Hoyt, K. B. *An introduction to career education: a policy paper of the U.S. office of education.* (DHEW Publication No. OE 75-00504). Washington, D.C.: U.S. Government Printing Office, 1975.

Hoyt, K. B., Evans, R. N., Mackin, E. F. & Mangum, G.L. *Career education: what it is and how to do it.* Salt Lake City: Olympus Publishing Company, 1972, 1974 (2nd edition).

Hungerford, R. The Detroit plan for occupational educationa of the mentally retarded. *American Journal of Mental Deficiency,* 1941, *46,* 102-108.

Marland, S. P. *Career education: a proposal for reform.* New York: McGraw-Hill Book Company, 1974.

Chapter II

Who Are the Handicapped?

 One could define the term "handicapped" in a wide variety of ways. One could say, for example, that a person who does not have sufficient education to take any job he chooses is a handicapped person. One could limit the definition of "handicapped" only to persons who have profound sensory impairments such as total blindness or deafness. Or, as sometimes appears to be the case, one can think primarily of particular groups such as the physically disabled.

In rehabilitation or special education work, the term "handicapped" is often used to refer to individuals who have sensory impairments (vision or hearing, for example), or motor impairments (cerebral palsy), cognitive impairments (mental retardation or learning disabilities), or psychosocial difficulties (neuroses or behavioral disorders). It might be more accurate to use the term "disabled" to refer to such persons, the distinction being one which can be important for vocational planning. The term "disabled" is used to refer to individuals who have been classified as mentally retarded, educationally handicapped, visually impaired, hearing impaired, deaf, blind, emotionally disturbed, mentally ill, physically handicapped, cerebral palsied, chronically ill, learning disabled, socially maladjusted, delinquent, emotionally maladjusted, aphasic, Strauss syndrome, brain injured, perceptually handicapped, quadriplegic, midget, cleft palate, psychotic, epileptic, mentally deficient, or socially maladjusted.

In addition, some individuals in professions would include those persons who are prevented from reaching their potential because of such social disadvantages as inadequate income for the family or inappropriate childrearing on the part of the parents, and those from sub-cultures against which discrimination has been practiced.

Despite the fact that many individuals with sensory-motor, cognitive or psychosocial problems do have greater difficulty in preparing for and functioning in the world of work, it has been frequently demonstrated that such persons can function in many jobs as well as or better than "normal" individuals. A blind judge may conduct court, a youngster who was learning-disabled as a child may become a physician, a deaf man may write novels, a retarded woman may function well as a nurse's aide.

And then there are stories of famous persons who were handicapped as children or were famous despite their handicaps. They tell us that Julius Caesar was epileptic. Beethoven became deaf. Thomas Edison had a serious hearing handicap. Helen Keller was both blind and deaf. Franklin Delano Roosevelt had a severe motor impairment following infantile paralysis. Biographers tell us that John F. Kennedy had a chronic illness known as Addison's disease. Some say that Daniel Webster had been afflicted with hydrocephalus. Some organizations which are lobbying for better educational programs and better occupational opportunities for children with learning disabilities report that a well-known president's daughter, the Governor of one of our largest states, and a British prime minister had a learning disability as children. If the reports of learning disability were accurate, these individuals may have been handicapped in some ways but not others. The famous blind rock singer is probably handicapped in the sense that he is unable to read music in the usual form but he is clearly not handicapped to the point of being unable to earn a living, one far greater than the income of most persons reading these words. President Roosevelt was clearly at a marked disadvantage in being unable to walk but the poliomyelitis apparently did not damage his thinking powers. Nevertheless, getting from a wheelchair to a car, attempting to stand to address audiences, and even the simple matter of getting across a room, posed major difficulties for him. Clearly, the person who is completely unable to walk and who must attempt to function in a society designed for those who can walk, will be at a marked disadvantage and thus handicapped to some extent.

Rather than asking who are the people who are handicapped, we might better ask ourselves questions concerning the degree to which a particular disability is handicapping in the world of work. Some disabilities are more handicapping than others. A disability may be handicapping for some activities and not for others.

Injuries, Impairments, Differences

An injury, an impairment or a difference may be disabling. The difference of being extremely tall or extremely short (giantism or dwarfism) provide concrete examples. The extremely short person has difficulties not so much because of any impairment or injury to his body, but because the world in which he functions is designed for persons who are different in height from him. Elevator buttons may be easy for him to push but his height makes them difficult for him to reach. The dwarf or the midget would not only be disabled in everyday living, but would be denied access to certain occupations because of his difference. The armed services, such as the Navy and the Air Force, as well as police and fire departments, have minimal height requirements which exclude the midget from these occupations. On the other hand, during World War II, midgets were in great demand to work in aircraft factories because their small stature made it possible for them to work in small areas of airplanes where "normal" size persons could not fit.

The difference of extreme tallness or extreme obesity could provide similar examples. In general, one might say that other things being equal (which they often are not), the greater the difference, the greater the disability. Whether one can overcome such a difference then may depend in part on the degree to which one is different from the general population.

Some differences are due to an injury or an impairment. Some may be due to deficits related to developmental defects, others may be a consequence of impaired functioning of the central nervous system, the glandular system, or some other part of the anatomy.

Impairment and deficits

An individual may have an intact organism which appears on the surface to be perfectly normal, but at the same time, have impairments in functioning. For example, it is extremely common for a person with hearing deficits to have no readily visible indication of a hearing deficit; the hearing handicapped person's behavior might suggest hearing problems but no stigmata, no unusual conformation of the ears, for example, indicates the impaired functioning. Hearing impairments can be due to damage to one of the cranial nerves which would not be visible to the observer. Another illustration is provided by the child with a neurological dysfunctioning; the body appears to be sound and healthy on the surface but the defective functioning can be demonstrated by various laboratory tests and examinations by neurologists. Such "invisible" disorders can interfere with development of normal vocational skills. The person with Addison's disease, for example, tolerates stress less well than normal persons. The diabetic person is more prone to developing other problems such as blindness. Other disorders which could lead to impairments or medical problems interfering with normal vocational adjustment include: peptic ulcer, petit mal epilepsy, hypothyroidism and hemophilia. Any of these disorders could restrict activities and interfere with functioning in avocations as well as vocations.

There are also certain deficits which are not clearly understood but which result in intellectual functioning that is well below that of the general population. Many mentally impaired individuals may have normal looking bodies, they may be highly attractive in face and figure. Nevertheless, there are some impairments in intellectual functioning which grossly interfere with learning to do some of the more complex technological activities that are required in the highly industrialized world of the twentieth century.

Deficits may include congenital malformation such as phocomelia (imperfectly developed limb), which would clearly disable one for certain kinds of occupations, especially if the affected limb is a hand or arm. The child born with a stunted arm does not have as broad a range of occupations available to him as the child born with the normal complement of arms, legs, fingers and toes. A number of congenital malformations are associated with head size and shape. For example, hydrocephalus may have a head which is much larger than that of the normal adult, especially in cases where treatment either was not begun in infancy or clinical treatment was ineffective. Another condition is microcephaly, a very tiny head. Both of these conditions are associated with mental retardation, although some hydrocephalic children develop normal or better intelligence. (The majority do not do so.) The microcephalic child, on the other hand, is almost always likely to be mentally retarded. Other rare congenital malformations of the head include craniostenosis or "tower skull" and macrocephaly, a condition in which the entire head and face are enlarged. There are other problems of milder nature, such as missing fingers, or unequal length legs. Such impairments sometimes make it difficult for a person to adjust to certain work activities. The world around us is made for people who have two arms of approximately equal length, two legs of approximately equal length, ten fingers set up in a particular manner, and two eyes set approximately half way between the chin and the top of the skull. Severe disadvantage is met by some persons who are born with a different size, shape or functioning of bones or muscles.

Injuries

An injury may result in any one of the parts of the body becoming either temporarily or permanently dysfunctional. An injury can lead to a deficit or a defect or a difference. Ordinarily, when the term "injury" is used, we think of some type of trauma; a broken leg, a lost finger, a damaged eye, a punctured ear drum, a damaged cerebral hemisphere. Although it is common to think of such injuries as occurring after birth, some injuries occur prenatally and thus the child has a congenital defect. Such defects often become impairments or deficits.

Whether one speaks of injuries, impairments, deficits, differences or peculiarities, these ways in which an individual can differ from the general population can lead to disabilities, some of which may be handicapping.

Disability or Handicap?

A small malfunction may or may not be seriously disabling. Other things being equal (and again, they rarely are), one could consider that certain minor deficits or impairments would be far less disabling than severe ones.

To recapitulate, one cannot look at handicaps in a simple "yes or no" manner. Whether or not a disability is handicapping depends in part on many circumstances, not the least of which is the degree of impairment present. Perhaps equally important (if not more so) is the educational and vocational training history of the individual with an impairment or disability. The degree to which the person has been able to learn and seek independent functioning, the degree to which the impairment permits independent functioning, the opportunities for obtaining prosthetic devices, opportunities for obtaining compensatory skills, the opportunities for obtaining an educational program designed to compensate for handicaps or mitigate the situation, all are factors in determining how handicapping a disability will be.

Among the factors one might consider are the development of attitudes towards work, aspirations, work habits, interpersonal and social skills, and a variety of other dimensions which might be subsumed under the term "personality." These may be as important as the physiological or mental difference. The degree to which a person learns to cope with the barrier-laden world around him is crucial. The desire to do so is also important. For some individuals, a development of a strong drive for independence would seem appropriate but for others, such a goal might be defeating. Clearly, the world will be too much for some handicapped persons to cope with adequately. However, there are normal people who are incapable of climbing to the top of a mountain or even to the top of a thousand-foot hill. Some apparently normal people can run a mile in less than five minutes and others may need fifteen minutes. When we look at the situation this way, it is easy to conceive of disabilities as relative to requirements placed on the individuals and relative to one's own wishes and desires. Although most wishes and desires are actually learned, they have been learned prior to the time a person starts planning for his life work, and so we must recognize and deal with such desires.

Ways of Coping With the World Around

For the disabled who cannot get remediation for the disability, there are basically three major options open:
1. One can deny the disability
2. One can retreat into the disability.
3. One can accept the disability and attempt to function around it or despite it.

Most persons with some disabilities use all three approaches to some extent. In selecting a vocation as well as an avocation, it would seem reasonable to take into consideration these approaches. The first approach can be illustrated by a person with a serious sight defect (but not total blindness). He could choose to use his residual vision in an occupation which was highly visual, such as photography. In the second pattern, he might choose to work in an occupation which does not require vision and where only blind persons work. The third pattern is illustrated by the person who chooses to work on a job which does not have stringent requirements for visual acuity but which might need minimal vision from time to time. There are some disabling conditions that make it virtually impossible for a person to choose the total independence coping style. However, a more common situation is one in which the partial integration and partial segregation is chosen. It is not uncommon for deaf persons, who have difficulty communicating with the hearing, to choose jobs, friendships and hobbies in which they can spend most of their time with other persons who are also deaf. If one withdraws into a limited world deliberately, then he may find more comfort, he might find much satisfaction, and he may find an opportunity to make a valuable contribution to the world of work. On the other hand, his options will be more limited than those of the individual who tends to interact with as much of the environment as possible.

Those persons who have a strong impetus to compensate totally, may find greater success in life. This may or may not lead to greater happiness or greater anxiety. Vocational counselors would probably encourage a middle course of action as the more appropriate adjustment pattern.

Handicaps

This discussion has suggested that many persons are not handicapped in their vocational or avocational activities if their choices are in areas where compensation is possible. For some other conditions, particularly severely disabling ones, the disability will be a handicap not only in vocational opportunities possible, but in many aspects of living. Among the disabilities which invariably handicap one are total blindness, deafness, serious mental impairment, and serious motor involvement. It may be helpful to provide accepted definitions of some of the more common disabilities.

What Are Disabling Conditions?

The disabled, with whom special educators are concerned, is usually defined as "one who deviates from the normal or average in mental characteristics (e.g. mental retardation), in sensory abilities (visual or auditory handicaps), in neuromuscular or physical characteristics (cerebral palsy, orthopedic dysfunctions), in communication abilities (speech or language delayed, stuttering, articulation problems), in social or emotional adjustment (social maladjustment, emotional disturbance) or in multiple handicaps." Persons with such disabilities are those who vary from the norm to the extent that special educational provisions are needed or that adaptations in the environment are required in order for them to function. As adults, they may need special adaptations in the environment, such as ramps instead of stairs for those whose ambulation is impaired, magnifying equipment or talking books for those with severe visual impairments; as children and as students in training, they may require special education provisions.

FIGURE II-1
What are Disabling Conditions?

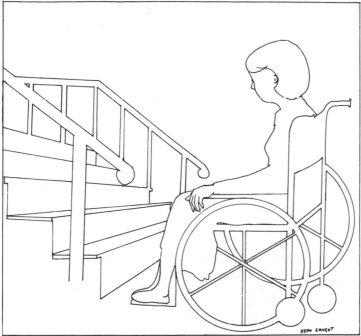

What is Special Education?

In general, special education refers to education for children with disabilities and needing some educational services not provided for in the regular education programs of public schools. The federal government definition (from Public Law 94-142, 1975) defines special education as:

> "The term 'special education' means specially designed instruction...to meet the needs of a handicapped child, including classroom instruction, instruction in physical education, home instruction, and instruction in hospitals and institutions."

The following definition has been proposed by Smith and Neisworth (1975):

> "Special education is that profession concerned with the arrangement of educational variables leading to the prevention, reduction, or elimination of those conditions that produce significant defects in the academic, communicative, locomotor, or adjustive functioning of children."

Many special educators today would add that special education is concerned with disabled adults also, when those adults need educational services.

Who are the Disabled in Special Education?

Many special educators make a distinction between disabilities and handicaps, reserving the term "handicap" for those disabilities which interfere with the individual's ability to cope with his environment (e.g., a regular public school classroom). A disability such as poor vision which is corrected by glasses would thus not be considered an educational handicap, the disability of color blindness would be handicapping in art class but not in most of the rest of the public school curriculum.

> Public Law 94-142 states:
> "The term 'handicapped children' means mentally retarded, hard of hearing, deaf, speech impaired, visually impaired, seriously emotionally disturbed, orthopedically impaired or other health impaired children, or children with specific learning disabilities, who by reason thereof require special education and related services."

Children with the disabilities listed would ordinarily be expected to have difficulty coping with regular classroom work in public schools without special services.

Definitions of Specific Disabilities

Professionals in the field recognize that many disabled individuals defy classification. Disabled persons may have combinations of sensory and intellectual disabilities. They may have physical and emotional problems. Many as children and some as adults, have speech or language problems in combination with other handicaps (e.g., most severely retarded and almost all profoundly retarded persons have speech and language problems). However, for a variety of reasons (e.g., research purposes, funding purposes, administrative purposes, to increase ease of communication between professionals) definitions of the more common types of exceptionality have been developed. They are included here as illustrative.

Mental Retardation: Mental retardation refers to significantly subaverage general intellectual *functioning* existing concurrently with impairment in adaptive behavior, both originating during the development period (by age 18). Adapted from AAMD Manual, Grossman *et al,* 1973).

In terms of measured intelligence on an individually administered general intelligence test, the following levels of mental retardation are recognized:

Mild: at least 2 standard deviations below mean (below IQ about 68-70 on tests)

Moderate: 2 to 3 s.d. below mean (between about 52-55 to 68-70 IQ)

Severe: 3 to 4 s.d. below mean (about 36-40 to about 52-55 IQ)

Profound: over 4 s.d. below mean (below about 20-25 IQ)

Adapted from AAMD Manual on Terminology and Classification, 1973)

Educators often use the term "Educable" for the Mild group, "Trainable" for the Moderate and some Severe, and "Dependent" for the Severe and Profound groups. *Note* that inadequate adaptive behavior must also be present and that the condition must be manifested during developmental years.

Hard of Hearing or Hearing Impaired: Sense of hearing that is functional (thus, development of spoken language is possible) but so impaired as to interfere with hearing normal speech. Using the International Standard Organization, the following levels of Hearing Impairment are recognized:

Slight: 27 to 40 decibels loss (in the best ear, corrected)

Mild: 41 to 55 decibels loss (in the best ear, corrected)

Marked or Moderate: 56 to 70 decibels loss (in the best ear, corrected)

Severe: 71 to 90 decibels loss (in the best ear, corrected)

Extreme: 91 or more decibels loss (in the best ear, corrected)

(Adapted from H. Davis & F. W. Krantz, J., Speech & Hearing Research, 1964)

Deafness: Hearing loss that is so severe that the sense of hearing is nonfunctional and the development of normal spoken language is not possible without highly specialized training (and often not with such training).

Speech Impairment: Speech impairment means some disorder of spoken language which interferes with normal communication. Speech disorders may be described as Articulation disorders (e.g., inconsistent or incorrect sounds, lisping, lalling), Disorders of rhythm and flow (stuttering, cluttering,) and Voice or phonation disorders (Hypernasality, very high or very low pitch, very loud or very quiet voice, monotones). Language impairments include delayed verbal communication aphasia, and multiple disorders.

Visual Impairment: Blind: Central visual acuity of 20/200 or less in the better eye corrected or field defect with angle of vision 20 degrees or less. Partially sighted: Visual acuity between 20/70 and 20/200. In both cases, definition means in the best eye as corrected by lenses.

Orthopedic Handicap: Includes such medical diagnostic groups as cerebral palsy, spina bifida, muscular dystrophy, poliomyelitis, and amputations (congenital or acquired). Many such persons have mobility problems. The term "physically handicapped" is sometimes used for this group.

Emotional Disturbance: This term has many definitions. The American Psychiatric Association manual on diagnosis offers these major groupings: Psychotic (e.g., schizophrenia, autism), Neurotic (e.g., anxiety neurosis), Transient situational personality disorders, Psychosomatic disorders, Organic Brain disorders. For educational purposes a functional organization might be: Problems of conduct or social maladjustment (e.g., unsocialized aggression, hostility, antisocial or asocial behaviors), Personality disorders (e.g., high anxiety, marked withdrawal, marked introversion), and Immaturity (e.g., excessive daydreaming, marked passivity, preoccupation, disinterest, sluggishness). These groups are listed in order of their frequency in studies by Quay *et al,* (1966).

Other Health Impairment: includes such medical diagnostic groups as epilepsy, asthma, diabetes, hemophilia, tuberculosis, trauma, and various chronic illnesses.

Specific Learning Disability: PL 94-142 defines this term as "those children who have a disorder in one or more of the basic psychological processes involved in understanding or in using language, spoken or written, which disorder may manifest itself in imperfect ability to listen, think, speak, read, write, spell, or do mathematical calculations. ...perceptual handicaps, brain injury, minimal brain dysfunction, dyslexia, and developmental aphasia." *Not* included in this group are those grouped under MR, HH, Deaf, SI, VI, ED, OH, OHI, or the groups sometimes presumed to have economic, cultural or environmental disadvantages.

As often used in the schools, this term refers to children with serious problems of reading, writing, or arithmetic despite IQ of 90 or more.

REFERENCES

Acts of Congress, Education for All Handicapped Children Act, Public Law 94-142, 1976.

Davis, H. and Krantz, F.W. The international standard reference zero for purse tone audiometers and its relationship to the evaluation of impairment of hearing. *Journal of Speech and Hearing Research,* 1964, 7, 7-16.

Grossman, H.J., Warren, S.A., Begab, M.J., Eyman, R., Nihira, K. & O'Connor, G. *Manual on terminology and classification in mental retardation.* Washington, D.C.: American Association on Mental Deficiency, 1973.

Quay, H., Morse, W.C. and Cutler, R.L. Personality patterns of pupils in special classes for the emotionally disturbed. *Exceptional Children,* 1966, 32, 297-301.

Smith, R.M. and Neisworth, J.J. *The exceptional child,* New York: McGraw-Hill Book Co., Inc. 1975.

Chapter III

Barriers to Employment for the Disabled

Disabled persons are consistently unemployed or underemployed. Statistics from the Department of Labor, quoted elsewhere in this book, document that beyond question. Guidance counselors and vocational rehabilitation specialists are well aware of the problem. One of the prime reasons for the existence of the support by federal and state agencies for vocational rehabilitation and vocational education for disabled persons is the difficulty in finding employment for them. The federal legislation on vocational education specifically mandates that at least ten per cent of vocational education funds distributed through the states must be set aside for training of handicapped students. A recent survey of the allocation of these funds indicated that a large proportion of the monies were spent on pre-vocational training for individuals designated as retarded (Olympus Research Corporation, 1974); some observers have questioned whether all the individuals served with these funds were actually handicapped persons in new programs, although the intent of the law was *to expand* services for handicapped persons.

Surely, disabled persons have no less claim to training for employment than do other citizens; the Constitution of the United States clearly indicates that disabled persons have the same rights as other citizens. This point is underscored by the fact that recently passed federal legislation (P.L. 94-142), a law that mandates that all states provide free public education to handicapped students, is designated a civil rights act by federal officials. Nevertheless, there has consistently been insufficient and often inadequate training and education available for individuals who have disabilities. Such a situation leads inevitably to underemployment and unemployment.

To know that the situation exists does not explain it. Perhaps some of the barriers to employment are quite complex, but it may be helpful to consider some known and some hypothesized barriers.

One might group the factors which interfere with full employment under the following headings.

1. The Disability Itself
2. Attitudes of Society and Employers
3. Education and Training Limitations
4. Attitudes of Disabled Persons
5. Economic Factors

The Disability Itself

Some types of disabilities obviously prevent certain vocational choices. The blind man cannot succeed at an airline pilot's job or as a portrait photographer. Deafness would exclude a person from selecting concert pianist as an occupation. Mental retardation makes it impossible for one to master the education level required for the professions such as physician, lawyer, college professor, or history teacher. The paraplegic cannot be a professional tennis star or dance with the Rockettes. Even with compensatory aid such as readers for the blind and sign language translators for the deaf, there is no possibility of their obtaining some jobs. Lesser disabilities also make certain jobs unwise choices. An individual with a severe nystagmus might be able to master photography, but be quite inefficient at the job because of the long time needed to focus a lens because of the constant horizontal movements of the eyes. Someone with 50 decibels of hearing loss in the best ear (corrected) might learn to play a musical instrument such as a clarinet, but the difficulty in monitoring the sounds made would probably make it unlikely that the resulting musical performance would be of the calibre needed to obtain a job. In a wheelchair, one can play wheelchair baseball, but the chance of being selected for the Boston Red Sox team is nil. Other, still less handicapping and often less obvious disabilities can preclude certain jobs. For example, color blind individuals (overwhelmingly males) would have difficulty in jobs requiring color discrimination; such jobs include interior decorating, paint mixer, airplane pilot, or electronics work requiring use of color coded wires. Epileptics cannot be bus drivers because of the potential hazard to others. Learning disabled persons would not be good script editors. Dwarfs cannot make the team for the Knickerbockers. Women whose endocrinological problems result in gross obesity, uncorrectable, pose no threat to Raquel Welch. Amputees are unlikely to be successful pianists.

Such illustrations may seem to place marked limitations on the occupational potential of persons with disabilities. In fact, "normal" persons cannot master the curriculum in medical schools if they have normal intelligence. The work of professional dancer, airline pilot, baseball player, clarinet artist, interior decorator, and master photographer will be beyond the competence of many normal persons. But the Dictionary of Occupational Titles carries 20,000 jobs. From that array, many are as open to disabled persons as to others without specific disabilities; a particular disability need not interfere with learning and doing some tasks any more for some persons with a disability than for one not disabled. Perhaps a listing of the kinds of occupations closed to persons with various disabilities may aid in clarification.

Visual Disabilities

Although the proportion of our population with total blindness is small, even severe visual disability can exclude the individual from occupations in which sharp vision is required to *perform* the job. Those jobs which ordinarily require vision to learn, but not to perform, should not be closed to blind persons. Since much classroom work depends on vision, it is not uncommon to encounter persons who assume that educational programs which usually require many hours of "hitting the books in the dormitory at night" should not be suggested for blind persons. However, the use of readers, talking books, and memory training may help to overcome such obstacles. Thus, one finds blind teachers, lawyers, and social workers. A recent report of a young blind man completing medical school at Temple University indicates that even the title of physician is not impossible for a blind person, even though much medical training actually requires direct vision of specimens. Performance in the role of physician, in most medical work, does require vision. The rationale for medical school training in this case was that the young man wished to be a psychiatrist and that that medical role depends less heavily on vision than does the role of surgeon, pediatrician or dermatologist. (One must wonder, however, in this case why the student did not elect to become a psychiatric social worker or clinical psychologist, both jobs that could have been learned with much less visual problem and both likely to perform many tasks similar to those of the psychiatrist, and for private practitioners, almost as remunerative.) To state a truism, persons with serious visual defects that cannot be corrected by surgery or eyeglasses will be at a marked disadvantage in occupations that require at least average vision.

In addition to visual acuity problems, there are other visual problems that can interfere with job performance. Among these are convergence problems, nystagmus, tunnel vision, loss of sight in one eye (interfering with depth vision), and strabismus. Each of these carries some type of difficulty that would make some types of visually dependent jobs inappropriate.

Hearing Impairments

Deafness also is rare, having an incidence of well under one half of one per cent of the population; it, however, is a clear deterrent to jobs re-

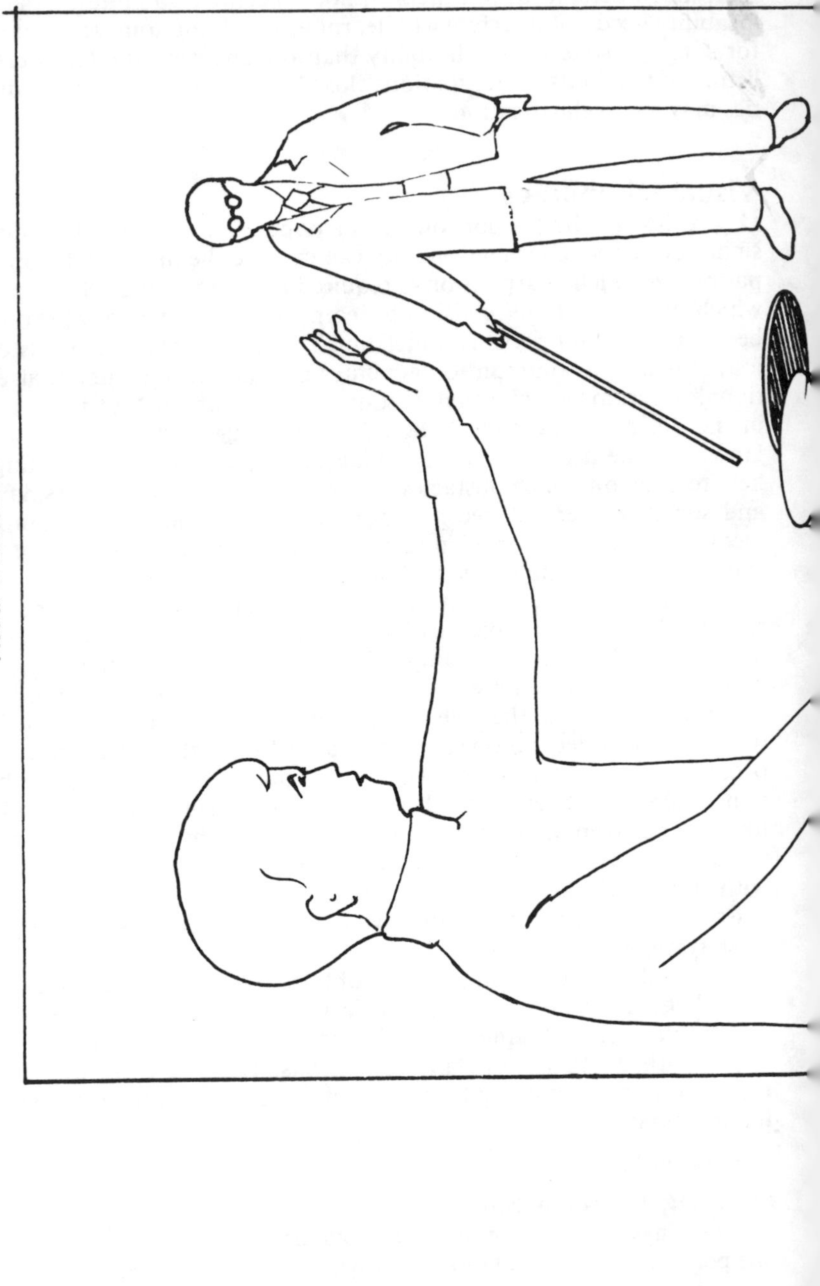

FIGURE III-1
Visual Disabilities

quiring good auditory acuity. It is also a marked disadvantage in jobs that require much vocal communication with normally hearing persons. Congenitally deaf persons rarely learn to speak in normal voices and their speech, despite the efforts of teachers of the deaf, is often extremely difficult to understand. Many deaf persons, particularly those of average or above average intelligence, become highly competent lip readers and can communicate with normally hearing persons through writing; conversations tend to deteriorate when one person writes and the other talks, but communication is possible and useful for practical purposes. Those with hearing loss that permits understanding of speech range are far less handicapped, although jobs requiring hearing of noises outside the speech range would still be closed to them. Thus, one with high pitch losses would be unable to perform as a piano tuner.

Although laymen often say that if they had to have a sensory handicap, they would prefer blindness to deafness, in practice the blind person is far more handicapped in an environment built for the sighted than is the deaf person in an environment built for the hearing. A far greater range of occupations is possible for the deaf person than for the blind one. A major complication in employment for those with severe hearing loss is the communication barrier; this prohibits them from getting jobs that they might do well at, because they cannot interact with fellow employees and supervisors through speech. Another problem for persons with partial hearing loss is the "invisibility" of the disability. Blind persons often are easy to recognize because of the physical features of their eyes, their behaviors which can make it quickly apparent that they do not see, and by such visible indications as white canes or guide dogs. With hearing handicapped persons, there are fewer visible signs and some of them choose not to wear hearing aids, which would indicate to others that there is a hearing problem. (However, one well known college professor used to wear a hearing aid device in his ear and let the wire hang in front of the ear and down the front of his traditional tweed jacket, even though he did not carry the hearing aid to which the wire should have been attached. This visible symbol of hearing loss telegraphed to his colleagues that he did not hear well. Consequently, all spoke to him in voices sufficiently loud for him to hear.) When a person's hearing loss is not great and he interacts in everyday life with persons who do not know of the hearing disability, it is not uncommon for his colleagues to assume that the deaf person is "stupid" or "peculiar" because some of his responses to verbal communications are inappropriate. He just fails to correctly perceive the communication. This situation can be detrimental to performance on the job.

Learning Problems

Learning problems can pose a variety of barriers to employment. Some individuals are so impaired that they are unable to perform complex tasks because they do not understand them or because they are unable to perform the problem solving tasks associated with the job. This is particularly true for the more seriously retarded persons. However, there

FIGURE III-2
Within the Individual

are individuals who are not retarded, but who have serious problems in reading or arithmetic; as school children, such individuals have been designated as Learning Disabled, Perceptually Handicapped, Neurologically Impaired, or as having Minimal Brain Dysfunction.

If the task to be performed does not require reading or numerical functioning, but the training for the task does, it is possible to devise ways of providing the training in ways that circumvent the learning disability; this can be done by using talking books, by modeling, by providing Readers who then make it possible for the person whose reading is very poor to learn through auditory channels. When it is possible to compensate for the reading problems, then the Learning Disabled person may learn such subjects as geography, psychology, political science, history, or geology as well as others with the same intellectual level; in general, Learning Disabled persons are of average or higher intellectual ability, but seem to have specific problems in certain areas of basic academic skills, particularly reading. For many, it is possible to improve reading so that they develop sufficient reading skill to function in jobs that are not heavily dependent on reading. Even so, their occupational opportunities are limited by their disability.

Mentally retarded persons vary in the level of tasks they can perform. By definition, however, they will not be capable of handling vocational tasks that require high level abstract thinking. Usually, the retarded (those designated as Mildly Retarded, sometimes called Educable Retarded, who function within the IQ range from about 55 to 75, and have also some impairment in adaptive behavior), are quite capable of performing semi-skilled work. Many of them can work as "helpers" to skilled workers such as carpenters, bakers, surveyors, homemakers, office workers. They work as busboys, dishwashers (including handling automatic dishwashers in restaurants), in greenhouses, on farms, on assembly lines, in furniture building and repairing, and on a variety of other jobs where high intelligence is not necessarily required. One should not assume that all who work at such jobs are retarded, but only that the Educable Retarded have sufficient ability to learn and perform those tasks.

For the Moderately Retarded, sometimes called Trainable Retarded, the job picture is less bright. In general, they are unlikely to be able to function in competitive employment in any but the simplest jobs. Usually they will need supervision on the job much of the time. The intellectual functioning for this group is from about 35 to about 55, and they generally have greater impairment in adaptive behaviors than the Educable; that is, they are less able to cope with the problems of everyday life such as personal independence, travel, and communication, with a majority of them having speech problems as well as limited vocabulary. This group is quite small, but recent efforts to provide them with their legal and civil rights has led to a strong effort to integrate them into the job market. From about 20 to 30 per cent of them are able to work in simple jobs outside sheltered workshops and about the same number or slightly more, can function adequately in sheltered workshops where the tasks are simple and routine, and are often done on a contract basis from industry. Examples of sheltered workshop tasks are: placing labelling stickers on packages; sorting and packaging nuts and bolts; assembling components of mechanical devices; replacing ear tips on earphones for airlines; packaging toys; and checking pre-packaged foods to determine whether particular batches are still usable.

One might view this situation as one that is inherent in society. Almost all of us have limitations on the level of job we can perform. Only a fraction of one per cent of the population has the intellectual functioning needed to understand and develop theories in physics, less than 15 per cent have the level needed to master the curricula and perform adequately as physicians, lawyers, philosophers, physical chemists, geneticists, or social scientists. Probably no more than 50 per cent can master the training and function as highly skilled workers. The difference between retarded persons and the rest of us is, then, that their options are more limited.

Physically Handicapped

The degree to which a physical disability is handicapping in vocations depends on the type of disability and the degree of disability. Many individuals who are in wheelchairs are quite competent to perform tasks which do not require them to stand or use their feet. Many with one arm immobilized or incompletely functioning can perform a wide variety of tasks that do not require two arms. Examples are: teacher, editor, insurance salesman, college professor, telephone operator, and computer programmer. One young man with phocomelia (one arm ends where the elbow would ordinarily be) has become a highly competent photographer. Even so, many jobs are not open to those with physical disabilities because of their physical limitations. Another deterrent to work for them is the difficulty in getting to the job site. Physical barriers to mobility are beginning to fall, in part due to a strong impetus from the federal government. However, stairways and doors too narrow for wheelchairs still make some job sites out of the reach of some physically disabled; the environment built for those with two working feet and two working arms is not always one that can be conquered by individuals with limitations in mobility. Since this area is covered more completely in another chapter, it is not discussed in detail here.

Mental Illness, Emotional Disturbance, Behavior Disturbance

The term *mental illness* is frequently used in our society. It indicates unusual behaviors, including verbal behaviors, that suggest disorders of thinking. In psychiatry, mentally ill persons may be generally classified under several sub-headings; the best known of these are psychoses and neuroses, with the former being more severe and devastating than the latter. Although the term "mentally ill children" is also used and there is a National Association for Mentally Ill Children, the term "emotionally disturbed" is frequently used for school children who have serious mental problems that are not primarily developmental in nature, as mental retardation is. Other terms recently used include behavior disorders, behavioral disturbances, and behavioral maladjustments.

It has been noted somewhat facetiously that there are two kinds of mentally ill persons, those who are miserable and those who make everybody around them miserable. There is a grain of truth in that somewhat cruel and flippant remark. Mentally ill individuals may be very unhappy; for example, those neurotics with high anxiety and feelings of worthlessness can indeed feel miserable. Those with psychoses, for example, can be difficult to live with and may cause great family worry about their welfare. Whether a person is called mentally ill, emotionally disturbed, or some other term that suggests marked behavioral differences and affective problems, his vocational adjustment as well as vocational training may be affected. It is not uncommon for mentally ill persons to work below their capacity, to have difficulty in interpersonal interactions on the job, or to find work situations quite uncomfortable. A few illustrations may make the point.

Ms. K. was a brilliant (IQ 142) and beautiful woman about 35 years old. She had achieved a highly successful career in the arts, written a popular book, and she had run a successful business for several years. At about age 28, she simultaneously sustained business reverses and an unhappy love affair, and was cheated in her business by an unscrupulous man. Ms. K. attempted suicide and was sent to a psychiatric hospital where she was diagnosed as paranoid schizophrenic. After several months of treatment, she was able to work part-time. Eventually, she became the efficient secretary to a tolerant and understanding physician. She worked well below her level of competence and training, but she managed, with outpatient therapy, to stay out of mental hospitals most of the time. One frequent visitor to her employer's office, however, commented, "I don't like to go in there; Ms. K. is 'always on' and she gives me the willies." Ms. K. was devoted to her employer, but unhappy at the job. One day when she was feeling depressed and could not reach her employer to talk with her, she made another suicide attempt—this time, successfully.

Dr. Y. was a pediatrician with fine training, a remarkable fund of knowledge in his field, and a "Pied Piper" with children. He had a large private practice in a prosperous town. Parents brought their children hundreds of miles to see "Doc Y." After eight years of successful practice, he had a manic-depressive episode and was hospitalized for several months. Efforts to resume his practice were too much for him and he had a second depression. Recovered, he took a job working in a governmental facility at a salary exactly the same as his income tax for the year before his first psychotic episode. After several other hospitalizations, he left medicine for a job that was less demanding, less remunerative, and less personally rewarding. It was simply not safe for a physician who alternated between mania and depression to take responsibility, and thus the State Board had to revoke his license.

Mr. V. was never diagnosed by a psychiatrist or a clinical psychologist. But he was neurotic enough to need one. His compulsive behavior was annoying to fellow workers, for he was forever setting their desks straight and frequently correcting them on minor errors. At home, he was tyrannical toward his wife and children, insisting that every item had to have a place and had to be in that place at all times, that the household must be run by the clock (breakfast at exactly 8:10 A.M., TV set off at precisely 9:30 P.M., tickets for trips and ball games purchased exactly 14 days in advance, fish for dinner every Thursday, cars parked exactly in line with the side of the driveway). Mr. V. complained vociferously when he was passed over for promotion to an administrative job. But his employers felt that supervisory positions required a more tolerant personality.

Once, one of the authors interviewed a highly neurotic applicant for a secretarial job; she used seven pages to fill out her application form, listing over 70 jobs for a three-year period. Her neurosis apparently had interfered with her job on each occasion.

Of course, not all persons with neuroses or even psychoses, have major interference with job performance because of their mental problems. Psychiatrists sometimes remark that there are many "walking schizophrenics" who function adequately at work. And many of the symptoms displayed by mentally ill persons are but exaggerations of behaviors seen in "perfectly normal person," whatever that expression means. The manic man is a caricature of "Life-of-the-Party Louie." The depressive is "Sad Sally" gone extreme. The paranoid is more cautious, rather suspicious Roland in the extreme version. A psychiatric ward displays to us visions of bits of ourselves, but in excess. Nevertheless, the "normal" individual may have a more successful and more comfortable job, better use of abilities, and a better work history than the mentally ill person.

On the other hand, on those jobs where there is little necessity for close personal interaction, and even in some which require it, some mentally ill persons do excellent work. Indeed, a mild neurosis may facilitate some work; for example, more than normal compulsivity can be a help in jobs requiring extremely careful attention to details. It is more important to note that a very high proportion of individuals who suffer mental illness at some time in life, may later return to the world of work and be highly successful. While a mental illness may make a person unfit for competitive employment during the illness, a history of having had mental illness should not bar one from work. In fact, those whose hobby is reading biographies, can name many famous persons who had mental illnesses. Van Gogh had what must have been psychotic episodes. It is said that Lincoln suffered from periods of depression. Nijinski became psychotic. Emily Dickinson was said to be a neurotic old maid. And one of America's first psychologists, William James, has been described as an unsuccessful, neurotic, young physician. The disability of mental illness may be handicapping at some times for some persons and in some jobs. But it does not exclude all who are or have been mentally ill from the job market.

Epilepsy

It has been said that epilepsy is the only condition in which having others know you have it is worse than having it. There is truth in that statement. Most persons who have seizures can keep their seizures under control by taking phenobarbital or one of its chemical cousins. Unfortunately, in a few cases, the medication makes the person appear sluggish and may interfere with rapid thinking. Also, in a few cases, it is not possible to control the seizures completely with medication. Anyone who has watched a grand mal seizure can tell you that the experience can be disturbing, especially if one does not know what to do. In most cases, according to current thinking, the best thing to do is nothing. One should only attempt to ensure that the individual having the seizure does not run the risk of additional injury by falling from an insecure place or hitting the head on a hard or sharp object. For example, if a seizure occurs near the edge of a porch, one may place a barrier at the edge. Epilepsy in which the seizures are controlled by medication should not limit the job market for most victims. However, by law, certain jobs may be closed in the interest of public safety. Such occupations as airplane pilot or air traffic controller might be included in a taboo list. For fear of embarrassment, some persons with epilepsy may avoid jobs such as preacher, teacher, or actor. One who has had seizures but keeps them under control through medical supervision should have a choice from a wide variety of occupations. Among the jobs held by persons who are personally known to the authors are: college professor, experimental psychologist, laboratory technician, administrator, textile worker, writer, politician, salesman, carpenter, lawyer, sanitary engineer, artist, counsellor, secretary, auto mechanic, and assembly line operator.

Other Disabilities

Certain other disabilities may be likely to have handicapping aspects. Chronically ill persons may need to seek work which does not depend on daily attendance. Very short, very tall, very obese persons may have some limitations in job opportunities. Those with debilitating conditions may be unable to engage in regular employment at all.

However, the handicaps that are inherent in the disability are far fewer than is often supposed by the general public. Many of the handicaps result not from the disability, but from environmental barriers that may be removed readily. The environmental barriers result from the fact that we have built our environment to accommodate the majority of the population, persons with two working legs, two useful hands, two sharp eyes, two keen ears, one quite adequate nervous system, and enough strength, energy, and motivation to function adequately. In very recent years, efforts have been made to reduce partially some of the environmental barriers. Hotel elevators have added panels with floor numbers (but not room numbers yet) in Braille for the blind. Street curbs have been changed to provide slopes that accommodate wheelchairs. Sign language is being taught to large numbers of hearing persons, making it possible for them to communicate more easily with the deaf. But the barriers are not by any means all gone and the environment built for normal persons can be quite difficult for those who are different. If the world were built for those with one arm, or with four arms, then the "normal" person would be at a disadvantage, as has been suggested in a recent publication by Warren (1976), who suggested that because some individuals are different from the majority, they must make the difficult choice of coping in a world that is often difficult but exciting, or living in a less difficult, but possibly less preferable environment.

Attitudes and Discrimination

That attitudes and discriminatory practices are major factors in determining the career potential of disabled individuals is obvious to even a casual observer. Research evidence that supports this contention is available, but hardly necessary. Both positive and negative attitudes can influence training and work opportunities, whether one refers to the attitudes of others in society or to the viewpoint of the disabled individual. A strong determination to succeed, appropriately high aspirations, and understanding of the importance of contributing labor in an intradependent society will, in large measure, determine the degree to which an individual may strive toward career opportunities in the face of the handicap of disability.

Within the Individual

Individuals, disabled or not, *learn* their attitudes toward themselves and society. Such learning can have profound, lifelong effects. One who learns to live with adversity and to cope with it may show remarkable efforts in the struggle toward a productive career. Cases described in published documents help to illustrate the point.

Christy Brown lived in Wales. As a child with severe cerebral palsy he had only minimal communicative skills and almost no control over his muscles. Without speech he lived in a lonely world. He could not express his thoughts by either language or gestures, but his powers of observation were well developed. His family were loving and supportive but they did not have the skills needed to teach the child. Fortunately for him, a few gifted and dedicated teachers found a way to communicate with the severely handicapped boy. Eventually, a system was devised that made it possible for him to use one toe, of which he had reasonably good voluntary control, to type out his thoughts. As an adult Brown wrote an autobiography, *My Left Foot,* and an autobiographical novel, *Down All the Days.* In addition, he published a number of his poignant poems. The tremendous labor involved in typing a book by using only one toe can be appreciated by those who have struggled with book writing, or even with term papers. How Brown came by his determination is not easy to understand. Development of such motivation, work habits, and perseverance probably depend on complex factors. In this case, the strong support of

FIGURE III-3

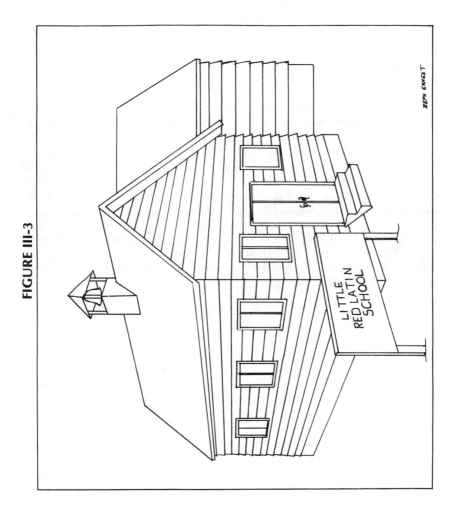

his family, the labor of his teachers, and probably the accepting ways of those in his small Welsh village were doubtless important factors.

Christy Brown was able to have a successful writing career despite his terrible handicap, the absence of skilled educators, and the additional burden of family poverty. One who came from a privileged family and had tremendous aid in overcoming his disability was Peter Putnam. According to his autobiography, *Keep Your Head Up, Mr. Putnam,* he apparently suffered a deep depression when he was a college student. A suicidal attempt with a pistol left him totally blind as a young man. Putnam recounts his struggle to learn to live again. Not only did Putnam return to college, but he went on to obtain a Ph.D. in history. His insistence on learning to snow ski despite the great handicap blindness poses in that sport suggests that he was willing to expend enormous effort and risk considerable danger in order to participate fully in avocations as well as his vocation. Many readers may question whether skiing is an appropriate activity for blind persons because of the considerable risk not only to the blind skier but to others on the slopes. After all, there are dozens of other less risky sports and millions of people live in ski areas without ever venturing onto the ski slopes. Although the authors are inclined to agree that neither snow nor water skiing are especially appropriate sports for blind persons, that opinion does not detract from admiration of the valiant efforts and strong motivation required for Mr. Putnam to learn skiing; we have both tried with less perseverance and less success to learn to maintain balance while floundering down ski hills with the important visual cues which aid in avoiding moguls and sitz-marks.

A number of famous persons have shown that a disability does not prohibit one from being productive and creative if the desire to do so is strong. Beethoven continued to compose music after he became deaf. Toulouse-Latrec painted remarkable work that was highly acclaimed despite his very short stature and deformity. The great artist, Van Gogh, and Emperor Napoleon were epileptic. Franklin Delano Roosevelt was a beloved president and George Wallace an active governor, despite their marked physical handicaps. Less well known, but highly productive illustrations are provided by a college president with phocomelia, a blind judge, a retarded young man with Down's syndrome (mongolism) who wrote a book, a comedian who repeatedly came back to a grinding schedule of work after bouts of mental illness, a famed blind singer and equally famed blind pianist, a deaf automobile mechanic, and a well-known novelist who continued to be highly productive until the day of her death from a progressive neurological disease. Less celebrated but equally valiant are the thousands of young war casualties who returned to continue their former careers or build new ones despite handicapping conditions. Among the friends and former students of the authors are an educator-counselor who became blind as a complication of diabetes, a deaf and a visually handicapped rehabilitation counselor, a physically handicapped and a blind secretary, a retarded receptionist, an epileptic experimental psychologist, a lawyer with cerebral palsy, a social worker who is an amputee, a retarded building maintenance man, an administrative assistant whose severe neurosis requires periodic hospital stays, a hearing impaired carpenter and photographer, a learning disabled television repairman, a musician who is paraplegic, and a professor who is a dwarf.

Christy Brown, Peter Putnam, and the others mentioned appear to have in common a set of attitudes toward work and life that facilitate compensatory behaviors which lead to productivity despite disability. Procedures for developing such attitudes cannot be simply prescribed. However, among the behaviors of others in the environment that appear to aid in developing the courage and perseverance needed to overcome disability appear to be the following:

1. Psychological support and sufficient protection by family, teachers and friends.

2. Avoidance of overprotection and dependency encouragement by significant others in the environment.

3. Efforts to provide prosthetic devices, medical treatments for those defects which can be remedied or ameliorated.

4. Carefully administered schedules of positive reinforcement for efforts toward goals.

5. Recognition of the reality of irremedial disability with concomitant recognition that each individual has unique assets that can be used for coping with life and liabilities that prevent one from doing some of the things that some others can do.

6. A broad range of educational provisions for students who have special educational needs because of disability.

7. Use of educational and training methods, materials and equipment that circumvent disabilities. Examples of these are the procedures of applied behavior analysis, analysis and sequencing of tasks into small sub-units, such procedures as recordings for visually handicapped and learning disabled students, electronic equipment, and carefully developed educational hardware and software (e.g. programs on teaching machines).

8. Community attitudes that indicate that the citizens with whom the disabled person must live and work recognize that "it's all right to be different."

Teachers, parents, and counselors are of tremendous importance in aiding disabled persons to develop patterns of behavior that can lead toward self-actualization. There are basically three major modes adopted by disabled persons in facing life, with variations and combinations of these modes used in different activities. The three patterns have been described in detail elsewhere (Warren, 1974) and will be presented only briefly here.

One pattern (which can be called the "Mole") is to avoid as much as possible those activities that require interaction with the "normal" world. For example, many deaf persons prefer to work and socialize only with other deaf persons, perhaps because so few hearing persons can use sign languages fluently and so communication between the hearing and the hearing handicapped requires considerable ingenuity and effort. Eschewing the "normal" world may provide comfortable feelings, but tends to reduce the individual's life space markedly.

A second pattern, far from easy and comfortable, is one in which the individual attempts in every way possible to deny the disability or that there is any abnormality. Such a person may attempt to do all the activities that anyone else around attempts, no matter how difficult the disability may make the activity. The illustration given elsewhere in this book of the blind student who was determined to complete medical school might be an instance. Disabled persons who adopt this pattern of behavior may be said to have chosen unrealistic goals; nevertheless, some find success and the approach offers the broadest possible life space. This pattern is reminiscent of the "Ugly Duckling" who tried (in that case vainly) to be a good duck. Like the Ugly Duckling who eventually became a beautiful swan, a disabled person might well find that it is possible to be a far more successful "something" else after careful and honest self-evaluation. After all, the world is better for both duck eggs and the beauty of swans.

A third pattern of behavior might well combine the more helpful of the other two patterns and probably represents the most effective pattern possible under disability circumstances. Where necessary, the individual avoids those activities that would be very difficult or impossible because of the specific disability. Otherwise, all aspects of life which are not related to the disability area are welcomed. The individual adapts to the disability that cannot be changed but does not let it interfere with other aspects of life. This pattern reminds one of the "Brown Bear" that participates fully in spring, summer and fall life, but hibernates during the winter months for which he is ill adapted.

One might consider the third adaptation the ideal. Certainly, it provides the best opportunity for good career or personal development for most individuals, whether or not they have identifiable disabilities. Some disabilities, however, are so severely handicapping as to force the individual into a very small life space. More unfortunate, others in the environment, such as employers who refuse even to consider having handicapped employees, may place unnecessary barriers for disabled persons.

Around the Individual

Instances of prejudice toward and discriminatory treatment of disabled persons are so obvious and widespread that one does not need to look far for examples. Despite recent efforts by the federal government and advertising campaigns, and research studies suggesting that prejudice is related to unattractive personality variables, prejudicial acts toward disabled persons remain rampant. Very recently, ramps have sprouted over college campuses and in industrial complexes where federal funds are crucial. Nevertheless, many work sites have invisible signs indicating that "No handicapped need apply." Complex factors are involved and occasionally prejudice toward the handicapped worker is seen.

Farber (1964) suggested a "social ambivalence" toward the retarded, postulating that a sense of fear and threat to major social institutions is generated by the very existence of incompetent persons, but he also notes a climate of sympathy and responsibility for the less fortunate. Interviews with over 2,000 persons in a large California community tend to support the "social ambivalence" hypothesis; however, even though there was ambivalence apparent, the predominant stance in that fairly typical community was rejection of retarded persons (Lewis, 1963). Zigler (1976), in a discussion of the problems of reducing child abuse, also indicated contradictions and conflict in society in these words:

> "Again I am tempted to point out the hypocrisy of a society (in America) that verbalizes its desire to stop child abuse but is nevertheless willing to countenance the legal abuse of children residing in physical settings funded with taxpayers' dollars. I refer here to the well documented abuse and neglect of children occurring in institutions for the retarded, hospital settings for emotionally disturbed children, and within our nation's day care system." (p. 27-28)

Thus, Zigler shines a spotlight on what might be called a "two-faced" society, but one that seems more willing to be rejecting or accepting of abuse of the helpless than to accept them.

A society is made up of its individual members, of course, and those individuals hold varying views. However, numerous studies of differing sub-groups in our society clearly indicate that a large number of our citizens tend to avoid or reject individuals with disabilities and employers may tend to offer flimsy explanations for failure to employ the handicapped. For example, Gardner & Warren (1976), reported vague explanations given by employers for not hiring physically handicapped persons; they also found an unemployment rate many times the national one. One might assume from the research indicating rejection that during depressions or recessions, the handicapped might be among the first to receive "pink slips." However, the evidence available does not support such an assumption at this time. Explanation for this might be found in the probability that only the better workers are employed and these persons, like other minority group workers, may "try harder" on the job.

Educational Barriers

In times past and in different cultures, the problem of education of disabled persons for those whose deviations from the norm were large was apparently a different story from that of recent years in the United States. If one thinks of education as preparation for assuming an effective place in society, then our histories and anthropological studies suggest that in earlier times and some other cultures, society has made possible effective contributions by disabled persons. In ancient times and in simpler societies, the practice of infanticide for babies who were clearly quite different made the question of education of the handicapped a moot point. Furthermore, the primitive state of medical science led to early demise for damaged infants.

Mentally different individuals have sometimes been regarded as very special people and given favored places as court jesters or court fools; blind philosophers have been revered. The philosophy of groups such as the Hutterites who live around the U.S.-Canadian border was one that provided almost no stigma to deviant persons and so they can function adequately without special provisions for education. In certain tribes in Africa where life has not been influenced by technological changes, there is not even a word in the language for such problems as mental retardation. The epileptic in some Indian tribes was given the high status job of shaman. Even in the United States during the first two centuries of the country, there was less difficulty for many of the handicapped persons. This circumstance appears to be related to the fact that the America of the early times, through much of the 19th century, was essentially rural and agricultural and the extended family of the times made possible absorption into the agricultural work force many of those whose physiological or mental differences would be greater handicaps today. After all, one need not know mathematics to be able to pick cotton or corn. Reading is not a requirement for separating seeds from cotton or grinding meal. Perhaps those with disabilities did not hold the high positions in the community, but they could do needed work.

Among factors that contributed to the present day situation are: the industrial revolution and concomitant urbanization of the country; the later technological revolution; compulsory education for all; and the increased proportion of disabled adults in the community that has resulted from medical advances that prevent early death of babies with some disorders. Thus, by the middle of the 20th century, it became necessary to develop wide scale special educational programs for exceptional children. By the last quarter of the 20th century, special career educational provisions for the handicapped were badly needed.

Special education for handicapped children had begun in a small way in this country with the opening of the residential facility for deaf persons in Hartford, Connecticut, in 1817 under the direction of Gaulaudet. By 1850 there are residential programs for blind and retarded children in Massachusetts. In 1875, Alexander Graham Bell was teaching classes at Boston University on education of the deaf. By 1900, special classes in public schools had made an appearance. However, it was not until about the time of World War II that special education programs began their rapid growth. Children with visual, auditory, and learning problems, and those with chronic illnesses or severe motor handicaps could not function adequately in typical classrooms created to serve the needs of the majority. However, by 1970, only about one half of the number of children estimated to need special education in the United States were receiving it, indicating that lack of educational provisions was a great barrier to employment. Also, there was marked variation in different state systems of education in the degree to which exceptional children received service. In 1975 the federal government passed PL 94-142. This law mandated special education services by the states, with federal government's assistance, for pupils who are mentally retarded, visually or hearing handicapped, or learning disabled. The 12% of the school age population to be served under this law will increase the number of pupils in elementary and secondary schools who will receive basic and career education. Since the new law is a civil rights act, the federal government has enforcement power of the requirement that states provide services whether or not federal support is provided. Since career education, with its emphasis on occupations, is particularly relevant for exceptional individuals, the number of career programs is expected to increase greatly. Thus, some of the educational barriers to preparation for employment for handicapped may disappear.

Vocational technical schools have, until very recent times, been unwilling to accept students who were of sub-average intellectual functioning, seriously impaired in vision or hearing, or in need of wheelchairs or crutches. In the past few years, there has been an increase in services, primarily because the federal government introduced a requirement that ten per cent of federal funds provided to states for vocational education should be used for handicapped. A disproportionate share of the ten per cent of the funds for the handicapped appear to have been used on programs for students labeled mentally retarded; it seems likely that some local education units used a broader definition of retardation than that of retardation specialists.

Increase in special education programs and simultaneous opening of vocational technical education programs to handicapped may reduce some of the educational barriers now existing. However, in-service training for educators is greatly needed and truly effective programs for the bulk of handicapped students cannot be expected until there is more trained personnel to implement programs.

Improvement Ahead?

Numerous barriers to the labor market exist for disabled persons. There are efforts to improve the still somewhat dark prospect. For educators, efforts to provide saleable skills for and develop appropriate attitudes in disabled students would appear to be a preferred approach. Educators have far better opportunity to work with the student than to make rapid changes in society (although they have opportunity to develop attitudes of tolerance in young persons who will make up the influential citizens of the next generation). For the present time, one may expect some perseveration of attitudes of the present society and so it appears especially important to provide the best possible career training for those for whom jobs may be more difficult to get because of handicapping disabilities and societal barriers to employment.

REFERENCES

Farber, B. The sociology of mental deficiency. Presentation to the Study Commission on Mental Retardation, San Francisco, January, 1974.

Gardner, D.C. and Warren, S.A. Career Education Potential for Students at the Massachusetts Hospital School in Canton. *Resources in Education,* June, 1976, ERIC ED 117 454.

Lewis, J.F. The community and the retarded: a study in social ambivalence. In: G. Tarjan, R.K. Eyman and C.E. Meyers *Sociobehavioral Studies in Mental Retardation.* Washington, D.C.: American Association on Mental Deficiency, 1973.

Olympus Research Corporation 1974 (page 1). Summary of Report to U.S. Government on Use of Vocational Educational Funds for the Handicapped.

Warren, S.A. The distressed parent of the disabled child. In: W.G. Klopfer & M. Reed. *Problems in Psychotherapy: an eclectic approach.* (Hemisphere Press). New York: John Wiley & Sons, 1974.

Warren, S.A. Whither Goest Thou? *Mental Retardation,* 1976, 14(2), 2.

Chapter IV

Assessment and Evaluation

Everybody Evaluates

The simplest answer to the question of who does evaluation is: Everybody. You do it. I do it. All those you meet everyday make assessments of other persons and their behaviors. Evaluation of others is an integral part of everyday living. Every time you meet a new person, you "size up" that person. Your conclusions (or tentative conclusions) are based on your past experiences, either directly or indirectly. For an example of assessments based on direct experiences, consider what happens when you meet for the first time a person whose fingernails are extremely short and ragged and whose hand tends to tremble. Having had experience with persons whose behaviors are similar, you may immediately conclude that such a person may also have other mannerisms which tend to "go with" the ones observed. You might conclude that the short fingernails are the result of nail biting and that the voice tremor is related to "anxiety." Then, you may predict that that person may also be likely to find the taking of a school examination extremely difficult (because examinations provoke more anxiety), and may be likely to have occasions when there is shortness of breath and rapid pulse. These conclusions, however valid or invalid, are based on previous direct experiences you had in the past with other persons who exhibited a similar constellation of behaviors (or assumed behaviors in the case of the nail biting).

As an example of assessments which are not altogether based on direct experiences, you might consider the situation in which you meet a person for the first time and notice that the person wears clothes which are in a slightly different style from those popular today, that the person speaks English with somewhat different stress on syllables than is common in your geographic area, and has both a first name and last name that you have not heard before. Early in the conversation, you may ask the question, "What country do you come from?" or "What is your first language?" It is not usual to ask most new acquaintances their country of origin or native language. We usually assume (assessment again) that one is from nearby and has English as a native language. However, confronted with speech clues, name differences, and even minor differences in clothing, you may arrive at the conclusion that the new acquaintance is not of your native region. Here, we are making an assessment and drawing a conclusion on the basis of not having had experience with the particular characteristics before and therefore conclude that the person is a native of some other region than that of most people we meet in our everyday life.

Our daily routines are filled with assessments, conclusions, and predictions about behaviors. Driving a car down the street, you see another driver coming from a side street, see the light turn green for your street, conclude that the other driver knows the rules of the road, and predict that the other driver will have a red light and will stop his car. When a man gets into an elevator and pushes the button marked 17, you observe his behavior and predict that he will leave the elevator on the 17th floor; if the coffee machine for the building is on floor 17, you may predict that the man is going to get a cup of coffee. If we see a young man and young woman leaving a church, the man wearing formal clothes and the woman a bridal gown and veil, and if we observe others throwing rice at them while they get into a limousine, we are likely to draw the conclusion that they were just married. Then, we may even make predictions about their future behaviors...they will live together, have breakfast together, perhaps have children, argue about family finances, ...we may even speculate on divorce because we know the high divorce rate today.

In these examples, we usually make some estimate of the likelihood of our predictions being true. We recognize that our observations may be in error. The "bride and groom" may be rehearsing for parts in a play, although we would probably consider this unlikely. The other driver may not stop and so we often indulge in defensive driving, just in case our prediction that we can exercise the right of way may lead to a crash. The elevator man may not be going for coffee, but to another place on the 17th floor. He may even get off the elevator on the 10th floor when the door opens there. Recognizing the probability of incorrect observations and subsequent conclusions is not uncommon for simple behaviors.

However, when we make assessments of characteristics and behaviors, that relate to personality in general, we too often neglect to warn ourselves that such assessments are as likely to be wrong as those about drivers or elevator companions. The person with short fingernails and hand tremor: There is a possibility that these two are not related in the manner we assume. The hand tremor may be a consequence of some neurological problem and the nails may be short because he just likes them that way. Thus, on the basis of what you see, from your own knowledge and experience, you may arrive at conclusions and predictions different from those of other observers.

To pay attention to certain aspects of a situation is necessary in order to attend to those details which seem most relevant. At times, however, one fails to notice important details, or does not have the opportunity to observe them. In general, we attempt to notice those details of behavior that are relevant to our own role in the situation. We do not and, in fact, cannot attend to every detail. We do not necessarily note that a new acquaintance has hazel eyes, a few hairs on one side of the brow that are not in conformity with those on the other side of the brow, a blue coat with tiny red flecks, dark blue shoes with heels in good condition, five buttons on the coat, an ordinary watch on the left wrist, a voice that is sufficiently loud to hear. Nor do we always notice that another diner uses a fork to eat mashed potatoes, wipes his mouth with a white napkin, sits close to the table, and drinks coffee after the meal. We do tend to notice if the left eye is hazel and right one brown, if the coat is loud red, white, and blue checks, if the watch is on the right hand, if mashed potatoes are eaten with the knife, if the other person wipes his mouth on the tablecloth, and if a rare vintage wine is the liquid with the meal. We notice the unusual, the unexpected, the different.

Because we attend to those characteristics which are different or out of the ordinary, those individuals who have disabilities are more likely to have their differences noted than their similarities to others. We notice the person who carries a white cane for an aid in walking safely. We are likely to notice the different eyes and hairline and stature of the individuals who have Down's syndrome (mongolism). We remember the inappropriate responses given to questions by those who are sufficiently deaf to misinterpret questions. Sometimes the differences are so great and loom so large in our memories that we fail to notice the multitude of ways in which disabled persons resemble ourselves. This tendency of ours results in many difficult times for persons with disabilities.

Another problem for individuals with disabilities is that we also tend to group our knowledge. If we see a person with short fingernails and tremorous hands, we associate those with other characteristics of "nervous persons" and assume that the individual observed has all other characteristics associated with "nervousness;" then we may see the person as less "valued" than "normal" persons.

Nothing is inherently wrong with grouping characteristics, with seeing syndromes. If we did not classify, group, and organize our knowledge, life would be intolerable. The only wrong is to fail to recognize the importance of probabilities. All characteristics that usually go together are not always present in each person who has some of them. A number of investigators have demonstrated that there are about 40 different characteristics associated with Down's syndrome, but no single individual with that medical syndrome has all of these; in many studies it has been shown that all individuals with the medical diagnosis of Down's syndrome have intellectual retardation, but studies have also shown that within the group of Down's individuals there is a wide range of intellectual dysfunction, ranging from almost total disability to relatively mild retardation. The average person with Down's syndrome is likely to be rather seriously handicapped and unlikely to be able to compete successfully in the job market as an adult. However, some have been known to function very successfully in carefully supervised jobs and a small proportion may be quite successful in semi-skilled jobs.

An illustration from a disability of lower incidence, and thus one with which most persons must draw conclusions based on indirect evidence, may offer further clarification. Ordinarily, one would expect that the types of jobs available to blind persons would be sharply limited. This is generally true; vision is an extremely important factor in a large number of jobs. However, there are reports of several successful lawyers, many teachers, and one recent report of a blind young man who completed medical school. (One may ask whether the choice of medicine is appropriate for a blind person, but the fact that he could complete medical school is illustrative of his ability to master the materials and to develop compensatory ways of learning and that he is not in the stereotyped pattern of "the blind.")

When working with and planning educational programs for persons with disabilities, we must keep in mind not only the generalities we can make about persons from a particular disability group, but the wide variations within a group with a particular disability. One cannot make accurate predictions about the vocational potential of a person with Down's syndrome, blindness, or other disabilities only on the basis of what is known about the group of individuals who have that disability. (An obvious exception is the disability which can be predicted to shorten the life span to the extent that the child will never reach the age for a vocation. Such conditions are relatively rare, but the predicted life span must be taken into consideration in career education planning.)

If one cannot predict job potential for disabled persons on the basis of knowledge about the general characteristics of persons with such disabilities, what alternatives are there? One is to use assessment techniques which can provide knowledge about specific individuals and their characteristics. For all individuals, specific tests of interests and ability can improve vocational planning and counseling services; for the disabled, it is imperative. Informal assessments can also be very helpful.

Formal Assessments

There are degrees of formality in psychoeducational assessments. Ordinarily, we might assume that the more formal the assessment, the better the information obtained from that assessment. This is true only if the formal assessment (or standardized test) is reliable and valid. To use a highly structured test that has no known validity, even if the test is highly reliable, may lead to a situation in which the evaluator has unwarranted confidence in the "knowledge" so attained. If the test also has poor reliability, matters are likely to be even worse.

Validity refers to the degree to which a test provides "true" information. Reliability refers to the degree to which a test is consistent. One way of remembering which is which is provided by a simple illustration. Suppose that you want to make devil's food cake for dinner. You take a box of pre-packaged ingredients from the shelf, follow directions exactly, and produce a product. Each week for several weeks, you repeat exactly the same procedure, always arriving at the same product. If this happens, you have reliability. However, if the product you produce each week looks and tastes like and for practical purposes is chili con carne rather than devil's food cake, you do not have validity.

There are thousands of published tests on the market today and many more thousands of tests developed for research purposes. Many have reasonably good reliability but not as many have demonstrated validity. Those who make tests have far less difficulty demonstrating reliability than validity. To get an index of reliability, the test maker can split the test into two halves, get a score on each of these parts, and determine the correlation between the two halves. Or, he can give the same test to the same group of individuals twice within a relatively brief period of time and determine the correlation between the scores on the two administrations of the test. He can use some other statistical procedures to test whether a test has internal consistency. To determine validity, whether a test measures what it purports to measure, he needs some outside standard or criteria for comparison. One common practice is to give the new test and another older test which has some demonstrated validity to the same group of individuals and determine the extent to which the scores on the two different tests are correlated. Another technique is to find some outside criterion, such as direct observations, and compare results on the test with the criterion. (For example, a test of academic achievement might be compared with school progress as indicated by the judgment of teachers.) Efforts to validate one of the best known and oldest of the interest inventories, the Strong Vocational Test, were done by having large numbers of persons successful in certain occupations express preferences for a wide variety of activities and then determining which interests seemed common to each vocational group. Thus, with the inventory one could determine whether someone taking the test at a later time had interests in common with those already in the vocation. (The Strong does not indicate whether or not a person has the ability to do the job, although one may assume that there is some relationship between interest and ability.)

In considering use of formal tests, one needs to determine whether a test measures what it purports to measure, whether it is consistent, whether it is appropriate for the person or persons for whom it is considered, and whether or not one needs to know the information that may be provided by the test. Assessment "fishing expeditions" in which a battery of several tests is given to a group or an individual are a waste of time and money; they are especially unfortunate in that test use may give false implications to those whose time is misused in such test-taking.

In selection of formal procedures to use with a particular individual, the first step is to determine what information is needed. (What is the problem that confronts the person giving the test?) In many situations, an individually administered standardized intelligence test will be needed in order to determine whether a person has sufficient ability to master the skills of a particular occupation. Professional work usually requires relatively high mental ability, skilled jobs somewhat less, and semi-skilled work less; unskilled work demands lower intelligence. However, if the general intellectual level is already known, or if the vocation to which the person being evaluated does not demand much mental ability, then an intelligence test may not be warranted. Similar statements could be made about other types of tests or observations of varying degrees of formality. For example, in many educational situations, the family and home situations get a large amount of teacher attention. In some cases, family and home may be irrelevant. An example of this situation is offered by the practice in the armed forces in which little, if any, information about the family constellation is used when selecting skill training programs for members of the armed forces.

Formal, standardized tests may not be required in all situations. Other observational techniques may be more relevant for gaining some information.

Assessment and Evaluation

Relevant Areas

One can conceptualize assessment and evaluation as necessary for individual student prediction and planning, for determination of individual progress, and for determination of program effectiveness. These are inter-related and the same tools of assessment may sometimes be used for all three purposes.

Regardless of the purpose of the evaluation, the same general procedures apply. The first step is to determine if there is a problem and, if so, specify precisely what that problem is or, more likely, what those problems are. In an individual case, one might, for example, begin with the recognition that a teacher has noted that a student is not doing well in the regular classroom and then attempt to specify (usually with the classroom teacher) in precisely what way the student is failing. (E.g., academic work? Social adjustment? Work habits?) This phase may be quite simple in some cases, for example when a junior high school teacher finds that the student is unable to read the textbooks assigned. At other times it may be quite complicated, as in cases where there is poor academic work without obvious cause.

A second stage is to formulate some tentative guesses (hypotheses) about the factors underlying or associated with the problem. In the reading example given, one might hypothesize: (A) mental retardation, (B) reading retardation, (C) visual defects, (D) a behavior/emotional problem which leads the student to decline to make an effort to read the materials, or some other reasonable hypotheses.

Some hypotheses may be fairly easy to test, while others may be quite difficult. One might look first at the cumulative record to determine the feasibility of a particular hypothesis. Retardation is unlikely if the student has consistently obtained IQ scores around 90 on various group tests in previous years. However, if other likely hypotheses prove untenable, an individual intelligence test such as the Wechsler Intelligence Scale for Children—Revised would seem warranted because: (1) group tests may be influenced by a number of extraneous factors; (2) intellectual functioning does vary in individuals across time; and (3) clerical errors in recording or in scoring tests are not uncommon occurrences (Warren & Brown, 1973).

The procedure of problem statement, hypothesis proposal, and hypothesis testing will probably need to be repeated several times in the process of attempting to clarify as precisely as possible what is involved in a given situation and as changes are introduced into a student's or school's program. Thus, evaluation may be regarded as an on-going process rather than a static, one-time procedure. Furthermore, the process should be regarded as the responsibility of various school personnel, not merely the school's psychologist or guidance counselor. It may be necessary to involve various specialists within and without the school for evaluation of hearing, vision, family problems, speech problems, neurological functioning, other health problems or psychological problems, depending on the situation.

In career education for students with special education needs, three major areas of assessment of the individual appear especially important: (a) Abilities and Disabilities; (b) Interests; and (c) Motivation or other personality factors. The standardized measures and clinical evaluation tools for measuring the first two of these are better developed than the last insofar as this particular problem is concerned. Therefore, measures discussed will emphasize abilities and interests; attention to personality factors is given elsewhere in this book under discussions of social learning theory, goal-setting, work habits, and locus of control.

Abilities and Disabilities

By definition, students with special education needs will have certain disabilities. It will be crucial in planning vocational programs to have the best possible understanding not only of the type and degree of disability but of the available research knowledge about ways in which the particular disability is or will be handicapping to the student during training and on the job.

The assessment of most students will involve medical examinations, although it is often the educator who has depth knowledge of the ways in which a particular medical problem may interfere with training and work. Medical examinations may include general physical conditions and appropriate examinations by opthalmologist, otolaryngologist, orthopedist, psychiatrist, endocrinologist, physiatrist, neurologist, internist, surgeon or other medical specialist.

Examination by a speech and hearing specialist, language specialist, audiologist, or linguist may be needed to determine what factors may be interfering with or could facilitate communication and its development. Examination by a remedial reading or remedial arithmetic specialist may be important to determine whether there are specific areas of weakness or strength in basic skills. Physical therapists or occupational therapists may provide helpful diagnostic information, as may physical educators or recreation specialists. In many cases a social worker's evaluation of the family supports or lack of them is needed. Rehabilitation, vocational, or technical education specialists may be needed. Assessment by a psychologist who has training and experience with disabled students will be needed in a majority of cases. In all cases, a well trained and experienced special educator will be needed to aid in interpreting data from various sources and, for many students, to do additional assessments.

Obviously, not all or even nearly all the outside specialists will be able to provide useful information for educational planning for every student. In fact, the information needed is often in the cumulative record of the student and the special educator may be able to work with other school personnel to plan for a particular student without much additional information on abilities and disabilities. The important thing is to have as thorough an understanding as possible of the student's physiological and psychological strengths and weaknesses.

Some of the measurement devices that may be needed by the special educator or psychologist in determining strengths and weaknesses are listed below. The list is limited to measures that might be appropriate for students of age 12 and above. Although it is recognized that career education extends from kindergarten through life, career education for special needs students in elementary school may need to be little different from that for other students, especially if the classroom teacher is aware that the job market is more or less limited for the disabled and therefore ensures that job awareness and exploration units include jobs that are relevant to students with disabilities.

Measures of Intellectual Functioning

Only individually administered tests of intelligence given by well trained psychologists who have had supervised experience in working with students having disabilities should be used in assessment of intellectual functioning of students for whom information on intellectual functioning is needed. Group tests have their uses, but this is not one of them. Among tests which can provide helpful information are the following:

Wechsler Scales. Either the Wechsler Adult Intelligence Scale or the Wechsler Intelligence Scale for Children—Revised (choice depending on age of student) may be used and would be the test of choice in those cases in which the student has no disabilities which preclude use of one of these. These tests and their predecessors have been available for a long time, permitting many hundreds of studies on the relationships between Wechsler IQ and other factors. Each has high reliability (i.e., from about .80 to about .90 in various studies) and demonstrated concomitant and predictive validity.

Stanford-Binet Intelligence Scale, L-M. The first widely used test of this series was made available in 1916. Subsequent revisions and re-standardizations have updated it. It also has many hundreds of research studies that indicate the relationships between Binet IQ and other variables. Reliability and validity are generally good as compared with less well known measures. The Binet scale is less often used today than in the years before the Wechsler scales appeared. However, it would appear to be especially helpful for use with retarded individuals.

There are available translations of both the Binet and Wechsler scales in Spanish, as well as a modification of the Binet for use with blind students. However, the Verbal scale of the Wechsler is often used for blind students and the Performance scale only is frequently used for deaf ones.

Columbia Mental Maturity Scale. Developed originally for use with children who have cerebral palsy and could not take either the Binet or the Wechsler scale, this non-verbal test has also been used in recent years for students who are deaf or learning disabled. The research evidence on usefulness of this test is rather limited, reliability is not as good as for the Binet and Wechsler, and it has a limited age range and limited range of functions measured. Although it provides useful information, interpretation requires more caution than for Wechsler and Binet scales and so they should be used if possible.

Raven Progressive Matrices. This test, developed in the United Kingdom, does not require the person being tested to talk and so it is sometimes used for deaf persons and for others with communication problems. It is an intriguing measure, but probably is best used as a supplement to other measures at this time because of its limited range of abilities tested and the fact that norms on a U.S. population are limited.

Among other individually administered tests that may be used to supplement, but not substitute for the Wechsler and Binet in getting information about intellectual functioning are the Goodenough-Harris Draw-a-Man Test, the Peabody Picture Vocabulary Test, and the Porteus Mazes.

Adaptive Behavior Measures

Whereas the tests of intelligence are designed to provide some indication of what a person is able to do, scales of adaptive behavior are intended to give an indication of what an individual routinely does do in everyday life. Efforts to compare what one can do with one's daily functioning can be quite helpful in evaluations. Intelligence tests depend on direct measures, whereas adaptive behavior must be observed over some extended period of time or must be reported by one who has had ample observation opportunity. Furthermore, what one does may depend in part on what is allowed by the environment and significant others in the environment. Thus, a change in environment can readily affect scores on measures of adaptive behavior. The oldest of the well known tests of this type was devised to supplement data from intelligence tests. The best known measures of this type are:

The Vineland Social Maturity Scale. This is essentially a modified rating scale with norms. Credit given to individual items is based on data obtained in a structured interview with an informant who has had ample opportunity to observe the person being evaluated; mothers are usually the informants. Age range is from birth to adult life and areas covered include such dimensions as Communication, Occupation, and Self Help Skills. There is an adaptation for use with blind children.

The Adaptive Behavior Scale developed by the American Association on Mental Deficiency. Part I covers the same types of skills as the Vineland Scale, Part II is essentially a check list of problem behaviors. Developed originally for use in residential settings for retarded individuals, it has in recent years been adapted for community use in the Public School Version and is being used with students having a variety of disabilities. Age range is from birth to adult life.

In addition, there are some adaptive behavior measures developed for use with low incidence specific groups (e.g. the Balthazar scales for the more severely retarded populations) and hundreds of "hand-made" check lists made up for local use. Unfortunately, the "hand-made" measures usually have no reported reliability or validity and thus are of very limited usefulness. You are encouraged to seek out those measures that have reliability and validity because they offer potential for a variety of use. Furthermore, to paraphrase a wit, you are probably better off not knowing a child's abilities as measured by a poor test than you would be if you knew something that ain't so.

Academic Achievement

It is often helpful to know a student's academic achievements when one is involved in helping plan an educational program; for those with limitations it may be especially important. Most teachers are so thoroughly familiar with the standardized achievement measures in current use that details about them here would be redundant. For any who do not have such knowledge of achievement tests, the Buros Mental Measurements Yearbooks available in most college libraries and in many public school teacher libraries provide comprehensive critiques. In general, one can note that the specific areas of academic achievement that will be relevant for planning will be determined by the careers being considered. Some vocations require only literacy (about fifth grade reading) and others, such as those requiring university training, require competence in several academic areas. Among the most commonly used standardized achievement tests for high school students are the following:

Differential Aptitude Test
Sequential Tests of Educational Progress
Iowa Tests of Educational Development

Often, the evaluation of students in achievement areas will require the use of criterion-referenced tests, or of diagnostic tests. An example of a diagnostic test is the Diagnostic Tests and Self-Helps in Arithmetic which was developed for use in the upper elementary grades but could be used for older students who have problems in arithmetic. Teachers using this battery usually begin with its three screening tests to survey a student's abilities with whole numbers, fractions, and decimals or with a fourth screening test designed for use at sixth grade and above. If the student makes errors on the screening test, then one or more of the 23 diagnostic tests (i.e., per cent, division of decimals, regrouping fractions) is administered. There are available (See Buros) several diagnostic reading tests, such as those developed by Durrell and his colleagues. Such diagnostic achievement tests can be quite useful to teachers planning with students who will need at least junior high school level academic achievement for occupations chosen.

Criterion-referenced tests are useful for determining specific skills (or their absence). A typical example of a criterion-referenced test is familiar to most of you—the driver's license test. It would hardly be worthwhile to plan a program for rehabilitation as a taxi driver for an individual who could not pass a driver's license test. Fortunately, tests of this type can be repeated after training and if the individual reaches the pre-selected criterion, fine. One could use the driver's manual as a criterion measure of ability to read such signs as "STOP" or "YIELD." If the student cannot read such signs, either by recognizing shape of sign or words, then the first task of the instructor may be teaching sign recognition. At some later date, criterion measures may be used to determine whether the potential taxi driver can operate a car, make change accurately, and read maps. Evaluation in such cases is used to monitor competence attained. Of course, one could use achievement tests to determine ability or inability to handle numbers as required for making change and reading of street names, and predict on the basis of disability in those areas that the student has little chance of reaching the required level; in those cases, some occupation that demands less academic skill than taxi-driving must be considered.

Essentially, the measures that are often used in vocational schools in the form of work samples are really criterion-referenced or diagnostic measures. The validity of work-samples, however, is heavily dependent on the particular observer who rates the student; some ratings may include only ability to perform the task while other ratings, unfortunately perhaps, mix up skill with various personality factors. It does not really help the teacher or the job placement personnel to make remedies of or allowances for deficiencies when ratings do not differentiate knowledge of task from personal idiosyncracies. Therefore, those who evaluate work samples or performance in a short training unit are encouraged to be as specific as possible about what aspects of the individual they are rating. The single grade for a half-semester training unit is ill-suited to the task if one needs data on areas of strength and weakness.

Interest Tests

Interest tests have been used extensively in vocational planning for several decades and have been said to have utility for training purposes.

The best known ones are the several editions of the measures developed by Strong and later by Kuder. These can be used with normal persons, deaf and physically handicapped ones, and by others who can read well and use pencils. A few measures in recent years have been aimed at populations who have reading problems or at those who may be interested in occupations, especially semi-skilled work, that may not be covered adequately in the older tests. Table IV-1 shows a comparison of four tests to indicate some areas covered. Among those which may be of particular interest to those working with such groups are:

The Ohio Vocational Interest Survey. The developers of this measure used a data-people-things trichotomy as a basis for defining the world of work. Results are presented as a profile which gives a data-people-things code as well as percentiles and a scale clarity index which is intended to indicate consistency in responses. Among the occupations listed are machine work, nursing, manual, clerical work and sales representative. An advantage of this test is the attention to some of the jobs that do not require college training.

The Reading-Free Interest Inventory. This measure was originally developed for use with retarded individuals but can be helpful in studying interests of others who may not read well and may be candidates for semi-skilled occupations. All materials are presented in picture format; the student does not need reading for the test (or for most of the occupations covered).

Career Maturity Inventory. This test was formerly called the Vocational Development Inventory. It provides an attitude scale and a competence test with measures entitled self-appraisal, occupational information, goal selection, planning, and problem solving. It was designed by Crites to measure interest maturity.

Kuder tests. Kuder has developed a series of interest tests. The Kuder General Interest Survey (Kuder E), designed for grades 4 through 12, is a downward extension of the Kuder Preference Record—Vocational, Form C. It includes the following scores: outdoor, mechanical, computational, persuasive, artistic, literary, musical, social service, clerical, and verification. The Kuder Occupational Interest Survey (Kuder DD), designed for adult populations includes the same items as the Kuder Preference Record, but is scored differently; it has 106 scales for men and 84 scales for women.

Strong Vocational Interests Blanks. This measure has separate scales for men (84 scales) and women (81 scales). It is one of the earliest scales developed to measure interests and has been continually updated since 1927. It is designed to cover specific occupations rather than general areas. In general, it may be said to have heavy emphasis on occupations that require post secondary school education.

The Work Values Inventory. This measure was designed for use with junior and senior high school youth as well as with adults. Vocabulary level is about seventh grade. It was developed to assess the various goals that motivate people to work, to measure the values extrinsic to and intrinsic

TABLE IV-1
Comparison of Four Interest Inventories

SVIB-M	SVIB-W	MVII	OVIS
Writing	Writing		Literary
	Performing arts		Entertainment
Art	Art		Artistic
Music	Music		Music
Teaching	Teaching		
Social service	Social service		Teacher, counselor social worker
			Training
			Skilled personal service
			Personal service
Medical service	Medical service	Health service	Medical
			Nursing
			Care of people and animals
Recreational leader	Outdoors	Outdoors	
	Sports		
Agriculture	Biological science		Agriculture
Nature			
Science	Physical science		Applied technology
		Electronics	
Mechanical	Mechanical	Mechanical	Machine work
		Carpentry	Crafts
			Inspection-testing
			Manual
	Homemaking	Food service	
			Appraisal
Mathematics	Numbers		Numerical
Office practices	Office practices	Office work	Clerical
Merchandising	Merchandising		Customer services
Sales	Sales	Sales-office	Sales representative
Business management			Management
Technical supervision			
Public speaking	Public speaking		Promotion-communication
Law/politics	Law/politics		
Religious activities	Religious activities		
Military activities			
Adventure			
		Clean hands	

SVIB-M = Strong Vocational Interest Blank for Men
SVIB-F = Strong Vocational Interest Blank for Women
MVII   = Minnesota Vocational Interest Inventory
OVIS   = Ohio Vocational Interest Survey

N.B. These areas are representative, not complete.

in work, satisfactions that may be the by-products of work as well as those sought in the work activity. Thus, it may be considered as an adjunct to other inventories that typically measure similarity between interests of the individual being tested and successful workers in various fields of work.

Extensive discussion on interest inventories and on their selection has been presented by Zytowski (1973). Readers who plan to use interest measures may find that work especially helpful.

Extensive reviews of a large number of vocational tests, including both interest tests and vocational aptitude tests can be found in Buros' *Vocational Tests and Reviews* (1975). Many of the measurement devices described in that volume are appropriate for use with handicapped students and so those who plan to do evaluations with students who have disabilities would be aided by careful study of some of the hundreds of measures discussed in that volume. This volume provides a rich source of information, including reviews of research work on tests, a publisher's directory, and cross-index to Buros' *Tests in Print*. The reviews in the new volume are reprinted from vocational sections of the Yearbooks printed from 1938 to 1972. Denton (1973) also reviews tests.

Personality Measures

Hundreds of measures of specific personality variables, as well as a variety of projective techniques and personality profile producing inventories have been published in the past fifty years. Those which are most popular, such as the projective techniques and the broad inventories, require extensive training in test use and personality theory. To date, results from use of such measures with handicapped persons has not been particularly encouraging. A small number of measures of specific variables are promising. Discussion of some of those measures is presented elsewhere in this book.

In summary, approach to evaluation can be seen as a problem solving one. We must ask what are the assets and the liabilities of the disabled student and what avenues are available to successful adaptation to the world of work. In using measurement devices to aid in problem solving, we must recognize that tests are merely tools that can help us be more precise in our predictions. No test can provide the teacher with answers, but teachers can arrive at better solutions to problems if data from evaluations are used intelligently.

REFERENCES

Buros, I. K. *Mental Measurements Yearbook.* Highland Park. N.J.: Gryphon Press, 1938-1972.

Buros, O. K. *Vocational Tests and Reviews.* Highland Park, N.J.: Gryphon Press, 1975.

Denton, W.D. *Student Evaluation in Vocational and Technical Education,* 1973, ERIC Clearinghouse on Vocational and Technical Education, Columbis, Ohio: Center for Vocational and Technical Education, Ohio State University.

Warren, S.A. and Brown, W.G., Jr. Examiner Scoring errors on individual intelligence tests. *Psychology in the Schools,* X, 118-122, 1973.

Zytowski, D. G. *Contemporary Approaches to Interest Measurement.* Minneapolis: University of Minnesota Press, 1973.

Chapter V

Psychology: What's in it for the Handicapped? (Learning Principles and their Applications in the World of Work)

Psychology has produced numerous learning theories, some of which are cited in other chapters in this book. The history of efforts by American psychologists to gain a better understanding of human behavior began about a century ago when a young Harvard University physician turned to psychological studies and established the first psychology laboratory in this country; William James not only sought new understanding of human behavior, but attempted to use his insights to improve the skills of teachers. In his 1899 book, *Talks to Teachers on Psychology,* he made the following comment: "I have found by experience that what my hearers seem least to relish is analytical technicality, and what they most care for is concrete practical application." Thus, James wrote his book for teachers, recognizing that some of his colleagues would criticize, but also recognizing that technical analytical writing can be quite boring to many of us; and many boring books are closed without having been read.

Teachers in the last quarter of the twentieth century, unlike those to whom William James talked, have all had a background in psychology and principles of learning. Unfortunately, many of us as teachers have found that we demonstrate some of the "principles of forgetting" that we learned in our college days. Therefore, in this chapter, some of the better established principles of learning will be reviewed. In general, these principles will not be tied to the various theories in which they may have been used as building blocks. Those readers who wish to study psychological theories are referred to the nearest psychology library, where they can find excellent books on the topic (e.g., Hull, *Principles of Behavior,* 1949; Miller and Dollard, *Social Learning and Imitation,* 1941; Hebb, *The Organization of Behavior: A Neuropsychological Theory,* 1949; Deese and Hulse, *The Psychology of Learning,* 1967; Festinger, *A Theory of Cognitive Dissonance,* 1957; Skinner, *The Behavior of Organisms,* 1939; Bandura and Walters, *Social Learning and Personality Development,* 1963, and many more recent ones). The materials presented in this chapter will be less ambitious and will be presented as simple principles that seem to be useful in helping others learn job skills. We are aware that, as Bruner noted a decade ago, psychology has developed a plethora of theories of learning, but few theories of instruction. Bruner's book (1966) *Toward a Theory of Instruction,* and his later work are designed to remedy that situation; the Bruner work, however, is generally concerned with younger learners rather than work situations. We will attend to those principles that appear to have the greatest relevance to vocational training. The principles offered are taken from studies of "normal individuals," but as far as we know from studies of disabled persons, these principles apply to them, also, in most cases.

Perhaps the first and most obvious observation to be made is that one must never forget that there is a long history of debate and discordant findings in studies of human behavior. This does not mean that some investigators have been "wrong" and others "right" (although that is a possibility, of course). It probably indicates the remarkable complexity of the issues, the tremendous variability of humans, and the difficulty in designing definitive experiments without great expense in time and money on the part of investigators and participants in research studies. In attempting to apply learning principles in designing teaching programs, we must not mistake a set of principles for a magic wand. If there were sure-fire, absolutely certain, guaranteed procedures that worked every time, you would long since have learned about them and there would be no need for this chapter. In fact, these principles offer guidelines which can increase teaching efficiency if they are used with good common sense; they will not work magic. You are forewarned. Do not, however, fail to recognize that there is much to be gained by wise use of the principles or that most human behavior is learned rather than being instinctive and much of it learned through respondent (or instrumental) conditioning.

The Learning Process (Acquiring and Maintaining New Skills or Knowledge)

One of the oldest and best established of the learning principles was offered to teachers by the father of Educational Psychology, Edward L. Thorndike, in 1911. He called it The Law of Effect:

Of the several responses made to the same situation, those which are accompanied or closely followed by satisfaction to the animal will, other things being equal, be more firmly connected to the situation so that, when it recurs, they will be more likely to recur; those which are accompanied or closely followed by discomfort to the animal will, other things being equal, have their connections with the situation weakened, so that, when it recurs, they will be less likely to recur.

Thorndike defined something that satisfies as something the animal does nothing to avoid, often doing such things as would acquire or maintain the "satisfier;" by "discomfort" he meant an annoyer, a thing that the animal does nothing to acquire and often doing such things as would lead to the termination of the "annoyer" or at least to avoidance of it.

In the 75 years since Thorndike's book entitled *Animal Intelligence* appeared in 1911, and his 1932 book on learning appeared, literally thousands of experiments have investigated the phenomenon from one theoretical viewpoint or another. In the past two decades, those who are known as "Behavior Modifiers" or scientists in "Applied Behavioral Analysis" have used a variation of Thorndike's Law of Effect as a keystone in their work. Many recent entrants to the field of education have apparently been led to believe that the concept is quite new. In fact, James described it in general terms, and without the cat experiments that Thorndike used; the general principle had been used systematically for centuries to train circus animals as well as work animals. There has been considerable debate about whether new learning can be acquired without the initial actions having "pleasant consequences" or reinforcements in current terminology. We suspect that learning probably does take place without reinforcement under some conditions. Nevertheless, under most conditions, positive reinforcement (pleasant consequences *immediately* following a specific act) seems to be helpful in acquiring new skills. Therefore, this principle is offered:

I. BEHAVIORS WHICH ARE FOLLOWED BY A CONSEQUENCE THAT IS PLEASANT ARE LIKELY TO BE REPEATED.

Please note that the term "reward" is avoided because it tends to suggest that "something is presented" to the learner; in fact, a pleasant consequence for one person may not be a pleasant one for another; a pleasant consequence may be internal—a feeling of "success"—or it may be the taste of a piece of candy. Furthermore, what is pleasant at one time to one person may not be pleasant at another time or to another person. (If you don't believe this, try eating, at one sitting, eight slices of your favorite pie and see whether the eighth piece gives as much pleasure as the first one.) In current terminology, the words "positive reinforcement" are commonly used to indicate that a consequence is pleasant; *by definition,* a "positive reinforcer" must increase the frequency of the behavior it follows. So, if you have tried to use Principle I and did not get results, check to be sure whether or not the "pleasantness" of the consequence was firmly established or whether ir was merely assumed. If the behavior did not change, the assumption that the "reinforcer" was a reinforcer may have been unwarranted. Or, the time between the behavior and the pleasant consequence may have been too long, which leads to the second principle:

II. BEHAVIORS FOLLOWED *ALMOST IMMEDIATELY* BY PLEASANT CONSEQUENCES ARE MORE LIKELY TO BE REPEATED THAN THOSE IN WHICH THERE IS A TIME GAP BETWEEN BEHAVIOR AND CONSEQUENCE

And by "almost immediately," we mean within a second, not within fifteen minutes. The well demonstrated effectiveness of the programmed instruction procedures may be in part due to the immediate reinforcement available, as well as the knowledge of the correctness of the response made, which reminds us that:

III. IMMEDIATE FEEDBACK ON THE CORRECTNESS OF A RESPONSE (BEHAVIOR) AIDS IN THE MASTERY OF NEW SKILLS

Like most old adages, the one that tells us that "practice makes perfect" is only a half-truth. Immediate feedback provides the learner an opportunity to make corrections before practicing the "incorrect" response. With motor skills, which much occupational training involves, it is especially important to avoid learning wrong responses because motor skills are maintained much more readily than cognitive ones. To practice the "wrong" response and later learn that it is wrong can be onerous to the learner; it might even be a punishment for the learner.

IV. PUNISHMENT, UNPLEASANT CONSEQUENCES AND NOXIOUS STIMULI THAT IMMEDIATELY FOLLOW A BEHAVIOR HAVE VARIABLE AND UNCERTAIN CONSEQUENCES AND SO ARE GENERALLY BEST AVOIDED IN TEACHING SITUATIONS

Unpleasant consequences that follow behaviors do not have the opposite effect of pleasant ones, as might be supposed (and as originally suggested by Thorndike). It is difficult to predict what will happen when punishment is applied. Some studies have indicated that the threat of punishment may be a more powerful behavior control or modifier than the punishment itself, but even this is an uncertain circumstance. Some studies have suggested that humans can learn to tolerate a great deal of punishment without its affecting behavior if the punishments begin as mild and gradually increase. Other studies suggest that only very strong punishments suppress behavior and even then, the behaviors are likely to recur when the punishing agent is absent. (A worker who has been severely reprimanded by the foreman for the habit of leaving tools lying about will not necessarily be careful about tools when the foreman is absent.) In general, the application of adverse consequences following an inappropriate behavior is not very effective in the long run. Use of positive reinforcement for appropriate behaviors that compete with the inappropriate ones is more effective. Seeing a neat workbench, knowing he made it neat, may be a pleasant experience for a workman; developing this "secondary reinforcer of pride" may be more time-consuming, but it is far more effective than restrictive regulations and punishments.

V. PLEASANT CONSEQUENCES DO NOT HAVE TO BE TANGIBLE. A SENSE OF SATISFACTION IN AC-COMPLISHMENT CAN BE EXTREMELY PLEASANT AND POWERFUL

For children, and even for adults in some aspects of learning, it is very pleasant to receive something that can be seen, touched, tasted or manipulated...a tangible indication that someone else approves of one's actions. However, if all learning were dependent on a constant stream of rewards, then the "reward-giver" would need to be present interminably. Human beings, fortunately, learn to "reward themselves" with intrinsics (secondary reinforcers) which we call "pride in work," "feeling of accomplishment," "self satisfaction," "content," and various other feelings. These pleasant consequences are more powerful and more stable than extrinsic "rewards" provided by others, although most of us still need the approval of others, compliments from others, and extrinsic rewards as well, from time to time.

VI. IN THE INITIAL STAGES OF ACQUIRING NEW LEARNING, FREQUENT FEEDBACK AND FREQUENT PLEASANT CONSEQUENCES ARE NEEDED: LATER, THE LEARNING CAN BE MAINTAINED WITH OCCA-SIONAL REINFORCEMENTS

Most of us have to be convinced that a behavior really does pay off before we "acquire the habit" of routinely doing it. Afterwards, we may go for long periods of time continuing the behavior with only occasional rewards. (This helps to explain why temper tantrums are so hard to break; occasional rewards maintain unacceptable behaviors as well as acceptable ones.) Occasional reinforcements, especially if they arrive at unpredictable times, can maintain behaviors for long periods of time. Skinner once had a "peck-for-grain-trained" pigeon that pecked over 6,000 times without a single bit of grain.

VII. MOTOR SKILLS, ONCE LEARNED, ARE MAIN-TAINED FOR LONG PERIODS OF TIME WITHOUT PRACTICE

One of the potential problems in training a person for a task that will be performed on the job at some later date is the danger of forgetting. It has been well established in many studies of learning verbal materials (such as memorization of lists of words, poetry, prose, and associations) that the materials may be learned to the level of perfect recitation only to be forgotten within a few days (at least, much is forgotten). For motor skills, this is not always the case. Once a person learns to ride a bicycle, use a screw driver, assemble a bicycle brake, or clean a carburetor, the skill tends to be retained over months and years without practice. A small amount of practice after a long period of disuse can bring the speed of work back to the old level. Thus, in training for work performance, it may be very worthwhile to develop excellent motor skills even though the individual may not work at the task until some later date. Aspects of the job that require memory of verbal materials may need more re-learning if many weeks elapse before the actual job placement is made. Thus, more review of aspects of the job that depend on verbal skills will be needed than aspects that are primarily motor. (One trained in culinary arts, for example, would need more review of recipes than of shaping or mixing pastries.) Furthermore, for some learners, the motor aspects of the job, involving kinesthetic, visual, tactile, and sometimes auditory senses, may be more interesting and perhaps more meaningful to that individual.

VIII. IT IS EASIER TO LEARN MATERIALS THAT HAVE MEANING, FAMILIARITY, LOGIC, AND RELEVANCE FOR THE LEARNER THAN NON-SENSE

Vocational education programs have often been said to increase academic skills which were apparently very difficult for students in traditional academic classrooms. This increase in academic skill while working on a "real" job may be attributed at least partly to the fact that some of the reading and arithmetic, for example, in vocational training is directly related to the particular work activity the student is exploring. Material to be read can be seen as relevant to constructing a piece of furniture, baking, or repairing a machine. Many of the psychological studies on the relative efficiency of learning meaningful versus nonsense (unfamiliar) materials have used verbal materials, but the principle appears to apply in a wide variety of materials. The career education approach of job exploration may provide for meaningful experiences in which tasks and equipment are familiar to the learner. Thus it can be expected to result in very effective learning; having been learned in a meaningful context, the materials would seem to have relatively high resistance to forgetting, especially if the task and procedures make sense (logical) to the learner.

IX. IN LEARNING A NEW TASK, DISTRIBUTING THE PRACTICE SESSIONS WITH REST PERIODS BETWEEN PERIODS OF PRACTICE IS LIKELY TO IMPROVE PERFORMANCE; THIS IS ESPECIALLY TRUE OF MOTOR SKILLS

Many new tasks require repeated practice to develop skills to a functional level (e.g., typing, assembly work, driving). Studies of various times of practice, with various periods of rest, strongly suggest that for many tasks, especially those involving motoric skills, greater skill is attained by using several practice periods than by long, uninterrupted practice periods. For example, if one planned to spend a total of 60 minutes practicing typing skills, greater effect might be obtained from four 15 minute sessions spaced throughout the day than from 60 minutes of continuous practice. Depending on the task, practice sessions would vary in time and spacing; for some tasks, one half hour per day for six days on a particular task would be a wiser choice than a three hour session. (It is difficult to convince students, however, that studying a bit each night, with much of the time spent in recalling what has been read rather than rereading, is far superior to cramming all night before final exam day.)

X. HABITS, ONCE LEARNED AND PRACTICED, TEND TO PERSIST UNLESS NEW LEARNING INTERFERES WITH THEM

This is true of inappropriate as well as appropriate behaviors. To say it differently, bad habits are hard to break, especially if they have been over-learned (practiced much). From this principle one may consider ways of aiding a student to maintain new learning; for example, when a new concept is introduced and barely learned, it would probably be wiser to avoid introducing another new concept before the first one is very well learned and practiced; it is particularly important to avoid introducing a second and highly similar skill before the first one is well established.

XI. SOMETIMES A NEW TASK IS MORE EFFICIENTLY LEARNED AS A WHOLE AND OTHER TASKS ARE BETTER LEARNED WHEN BROKEN INTO SUB-COMPONENTS

Learning something as a whole has the advantage of increasing meaningfulness and indicating relationships between parts of the whole. Part learning offers opportunities for more rapid feedback on correctness of responses and avoids overlearning of portions of the material with the possibility of underlearning other parts. A combination of the two—some emphasis on the entire task and some on specific parts—is probably the most efficient approach. Thus, the learner can see relationships of part to whole and can have the advantage of learning small units, which is likely to speed learning.

XII. OVERLEARNING AND PRACTICE HELP TO MAINTAIN SKILLS

Materials and skills that have been overlearned are far more resistant to extinction (are remembered longer and better) than those which are barely learned. When one has learned something to the point of one correct performance, one may be unable to perform that task correctly next day or next week. It is likely that this principle underlies the educator's practice of assigning homework. All too often, the learner who reaches the level of one correct performance in class one day may be unable to do the task correctly when homework time comes that night. It is the better part of wisdom for a teacher to provide opportunities for practice and overlearning in the classroom before requiring practice in settings where no supervision of student performance can be provided. Once the student is fairly competent, additional practice can be very helpful in maintaining skills.

XIII. TEACHER PROVISION FOR TRANSFER OF TRAIN-ING CAN FACILITATE USE OF SCHOOL LEARNING IN NEW SITUATIONS

An old theory of general transfer of learning held that learning such subjects as Latin or Algebra would "improve the mind" and make all learning easier. Although that theory is now discredited, it has been demonstrated that training in one activity can aid the learner in some new activities in which there is considerable similarity between tasks. Students vary in the degree to which they can recognize such similarities. Especially students with mental retardation and perhaps those with learning disabilities and with "rigid" personalities can be aided by teacher guidance in recognizing task similarity. Generally, tasks in which the student must make a new response to an old stimulus will be more difficult for the learner than those in which the previously learned response is to be made to a new, similar stimulus. Thus, the student who has learned to turn a screw with a red-handle screwdriver will probably have no difficulty in applying principles learned when it is necessary to use a new screwdriver that differs only in that the handle of the new one is green. One who has learned to file materials alphabetically in a two file cabinet should transfer the filing skill easily to a four drawer file cabinet. However, learning to perform a totally new task with the old red-handle screwdriver or changing from filing alphabetically to filing numerically in the same cabinets could require some new learning before the correct responses are consistently made. This point was illustrated dramatically by an Air Force pilot who was provided with a modified version of a plane he had become thoroughly competent with. On the modified version, the lever that retracted the landing gear was put in the place previously occupied by a lever for opening the canopy. Sitting on the runway, he attempted to open the canopy, making a much overlearned response to an old stimulus (lever). The result was a plane sitting firmly on its fuselage in the middle of a runway in Gander. The pilot had learned about transfer of training the hard way. Teachers alert to the possibilities of positive and negative transfer of training can arrange for learning experiences in ways that maximize positive transfer where it is appropriate and minimize the negative transfer that interferes with new learning.

XIV. LEARNING BY IMITATION CAN BE VERY EF-FECTIVE

Learning new skills by observing another person is a complex and high-level form of learning that humans use very effectively. Speech, for example, is learned at least in part by imitation, with the result that children usually have the same accent (and grammatical errors) as significant others in their environment. Many of the tasks of such workers as carpenters, dentists, mechanics, beauticians, bus drivers, and musicians are learned by watching others perform. Much of our social behavior is learned from a model. Thus, the teacher who would have a disabled student learn simple courtesy, one of the most valuable skills such children can have, need only be consistently courteous to the student and others in the environment. If the student likes the teacher and wishes "to be like teacher," courtesy need not be presented in formal lessons. Modelling, however, is not limited to behaviors that are approved by Society. The adult who is unkempt in dress, argumentative, rude, or lazy may find some of the explanation for child behavior by looking into a mirror. Recognition of this principle may also help to explain the excessive preoccupation that some teachers have with "the home," especially if the teacher has a nagging suspicion about possible human imperfection of the image in the mirror.

XV. MUCH LEARNING PROGRESSES AT AN UNEVEN RATE

It is not uncommon to have spurts and slow periods while learning. With a complex skill such as learning to use a machine (e.g., typewriter), there may be fairly rapid early progress followed by a period of no progress, followed by another period of new progress. Such plateaus of "no progress" followed by additional improvements suggest that the original working methods have reached their limits and must be replaced by new, more efficient methods if additional progress is to occur. Eventually, of course, human limits will be reached but the wise teacher recognizes that a plateau in learning is common and works accordingly.

XVI. TRICKS FOR LEARNING AND REMEMBERING MAKE TEACHING MORE EFFECTIVE

Tricks for learning and remembering are sometimes called memonic devices. By whatever name, they help. Among the well known ones are: the word HOMES to provide initial letters for the names of the Great Lakes, a sentence used by medical and nursing students to provide initials for the 12 cranial nerves, rhymes such as "30 days hath September, April, June and November." All these illustrations use verbal stimuli. A wide variety of verbal mediators can be developed to aid students who have difficulty in learning. Reading teachers, for example, may tell students that the first vowel in a word tells its name (is a long vowel) if another vowel is standing next to it to make it do so, thus helping the child learn to differentiate "bail" from "ball." One can use "crazy sentences" to aid the learning of relationships, such as "your *right* hand is the one you write with and the hand that is left over is *left*." Other tricks include: painting outlines of tools on the wall to indicate the place for tool storage, using colored dots or markers on dials as indicators, color coding wires, painting a semi-circle on the back of a child's boots so that only when they are placed to fit the correct foot will the two semi-circles form a circle. The possibilities are endless and will depend on the situation. When used sensibly, they may make the difference between learning and not learning. However, the shrewd reader will have recognized that this principle is a close relative of others described, especially #VIII, and will attempt to ensure that the devices invented are truly meaningful so that they facilitate rather than interfere.

These principles are only a few that might be listed but they seem to have considerable relevance to learning work skills because they relate to motor learning as well as verbal learning. For those occupations that require large amounts of verbal learning, the principles of acquisition and forgetting of verbal materials would be important, also. However, for a huge number of jobs, memorization of rote lists of terms, complex principles or relationships, and complicated formulae are not needed. The principles on acquisition given here apply to most learning, both verbal and motor.

This particular list is chosen because it seemed especially relevant to job training, because these are among the most solidly supported principles, and because most of them are fairly easy to relate to a teaching situation. The reader is reminded that depth discussions of learning and principles can be obtained in any one of dozens of psychology texts, that there are likely to be exceptions to these rules, and that patience and consistency in applying learning principles make teaching easier.

To summarize:

I. BEHAVIORS WHICH ARE FOLLOWED BY A CONSEQUENCE THAT IS PLEASANT ARE LIKELY TO BE REPEATED.

II. BEHAVIORS FOLLOWED *ALMOST IMMEDIATELY* BY PLEASANT CONSEQUENCES ARE MORE LIKELY TO BE REPEATED THAN THOSE IN WHICH THERE IS A TIME GAP BETWEEN BEHAVIOR AND CONSEQUENCE.

III. IMMEDIATE FEEDBACK ON THE CORRECTNESS OF A RESPONSE (BEHAVIOR) AIDES IN THE MASTERY OF NEW SKILLS.

IV. PUNISHMENT, UNPLEASANT CONSEQUENCES, AND NOXIOUS STIMULI THAT IMMEDIATELY FOLLOW A BEHAVIOR HAVE VARIABLE AND UNCERTAIN CONSEQUENCES AND SO ARE GENERALLY BEST AVOIDED IN TEACHING SITUATIONS.

V. PLEASANT CONSEQUENCES DO NOT HAVE TO BE TANGIBLE. A SENSE OF SATISFACTION IN ACCOMPLISHMENT CAN BE EXTREMELY PLEASANT AND POWERFUL.

VI. IN THE INITIAL STAGES OF ACQUIRING NEW LEARNING, FREQUENT FEEDBACK AND FREQUENT PLEASANT CONSEQUENCES ARE NEEDED; LATER, THE LEARNING CAN BE MAINTAINED WITH OCCASIONAL REINFORCEMENTS.

VII. MOTOR SKILLS, ONCE LEARNED, ARE MAINTAINED FOR LONG PERIODS OF TIME WITHOUT PRACTICE.

VIII. IT IS EASIER TO LEARN MATERIALS THAT HAVE MEANING AND RELEVANCE FOR THE LEARNER THAN NONSENSE.

IX. IN LEARNING A NEW TASK, DISTRIBUTING THE PRACTICE SESSIONS WITH REST PERIODS BETWEEN PERIODS OF PRACTICE IS LIKELY TO IMPROVE PERFORMANCE: THIS IS ESPECIALLY TRUE OF MOTOR SKILLS.

X. HABITS, ONCE LEARNED AND PRACTICED, TEND TO PERSIST UNLESS NEW LEARNING INTERFERES WITH THEM.

XI. SOMETIMES A NEW TASK IS MORE EFFICIENTLY LEARNED AS A WHOLE AND OTHER TASKS ARE BETTER LEARNED WHEN BROKEN INTO SUB-COMPONENTS.

XII. OVERLEARNING AND PRACTICE HELP TO MAINTAIN SKILLS.

XIII. TEACHER PROVISIONS FOR TRANSFER OF TRAINING CAN FACILITATE USE OF SCHOOL LEARNING IN NEW SITUATIONS.

XIV. LEARNING BY IMITATION CAN BE VERY EFFECTIVE.

XV. MUCH LEARNING PROGRESSES AT AN UNEVEN RATE.

XVI. TRICKS FOR LEARNING AND REMEMBERING MAKE TEACHING MORE EFFECTIVE.

THE IMPOSSIBLE TAKES A LITTLE LONGER: USING DISCRIMINATION LEARNING STUDIES TO FACILITATE TEACHING COMPLEX TASKS

Much of the general public appears to believe that disabled persons, even those with mild disability, can do little. For example, in a recent report by Gardner and Warren (1977) it was noted that a group of college students, many of them special educators, had very limited concepts of the intellectual level or academic achievement level required to perform various job tasks. The task of assembling a bicycle brake, for example, requires no reading and can be done by a person with an IQ of 40 to 60. Yet 90% of the teachers in this study reported that at least some reading was required. Estimated IQ for the job was 70 to 100. Actually, there are a number of reports in recent literature, and decades of clinical experience with retarded persons in institutions, to suggest that with careful planning of teaching strategy it is possible to teach tasks that appear to be somewhat complex to individuals with very limited intellectual abilities (Clarke; 1976). We have long known that mildly retarded persons as adults can engage in a wide variety of tasks, particularly as helpers and aides, and others seem to "melt" into the labor pool, losing their identity as retarded. For some moderately retarded persons (trainable), sheltered workshop tasks that require simple counting, simple assembling, and matching are not uncommon. However, published discussions of training programs for trainable and severely retarded (but ambulatory and physically well) persons have in recent years tended to emphasize very simple, repetitive tasks such as object sorting, moving supplies, or filling packages; in a decreasing labor market with increased mechanization, many of those simpler jobs are disappearing. The labor market will probably not support any longer those with very minimal skills. Therefore, techniques to train retarded and other learning disabled persons at assembly tasks may be worth serious reconsideration. The procedures described below and taken from research reports may be used as prototypes for planning other training programs. In this chapter, use of data and theory from discrimination learning studies sets an example.

A major task of educators is to develop more effective and sophisticated vocational training programs by applying the best learning technology available for we must change the system to include *efficient* and *effective* vocational skill training for all persons with disabilities (Crossen, 1969). This is especially critical for the more severely handicapped worker.

An Approach

In our modern society, we are constantly bombarded by countless stimuli in a highly variable environment. One of our most common, and earliest, learned responses involves learning to discriminate between stimuli. Most young children learn visual and auditory discriminations, that is, the process of selecting the stimuli which are important for attention while ignoring those which are irrelevant. Many retarded and learning disabled persons, on the other hand, have difficulty in mastering this phase of learning.

Zeaman & House (1963) in a series of studies, formulated a theory to explain the difference between retarded persons and those with normal intelligence in learning discrimination tasks. Their findings appear relevant to individuals with learning disabilities and perhaps to other disabled persons.

Basically, Zeaman & House propose that a discrimination problem involves learning a chain of two responses:

1. Learning to attend to the relevant dimensions; and

2. Learning to discriminate between objects with different dimensions.

Zeaman and House postulated that the basic difference between retarded and normal persons in solving discrimination problems is not in a simple, single, basic ability. Rather, according to their theory, two processes are involved, the basic ability to attend initially to the relevant dimension (step 1 above) and then to discriminate objects and choose the "correct" one. If we can visualize the acquisition of a discrimination learning task as a "race" between a group of workers with normal intelligence and a group of retarded workers, perhaps the essential differences can be seen more easily as illustrated in Figure V-1, a model which indicates that MR persons require more trials than Normals to learn to discriminate relevant dimensions of the stimuli, but approximately the same time to learn that one stimulus is "correct."

FIGURE V-1
Learning a New Task

Attention to Relevant Dimensions

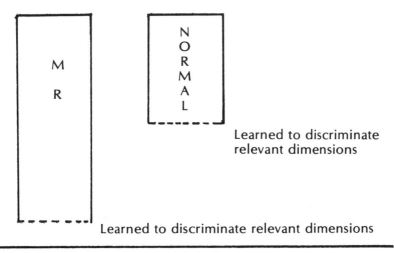

Learned to discriminate
relevant dimensions

Learned to discriminate relevant dimensions

Choosing Correct Response

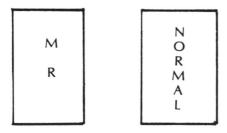

The difference is not in time required to make correct responses, but in the number of trials required to comprehend relevant dimensions. Once the retarded learner has identified relevant dimensions of the stimuli, learning the correct response proceeds at *essentially the same rate as for the normal person.*

The paradigm can be illustrated for an assembly task in which similar parts are needed, one fitting into the assembly before another is to be used. The worker must choose the "correct" part for initial use. Figure V-2 illustrates the point.

FIGURE V-2

Illustration of a Simple Learning Task Modeled
After Those Used in the Zeaman & House Studies

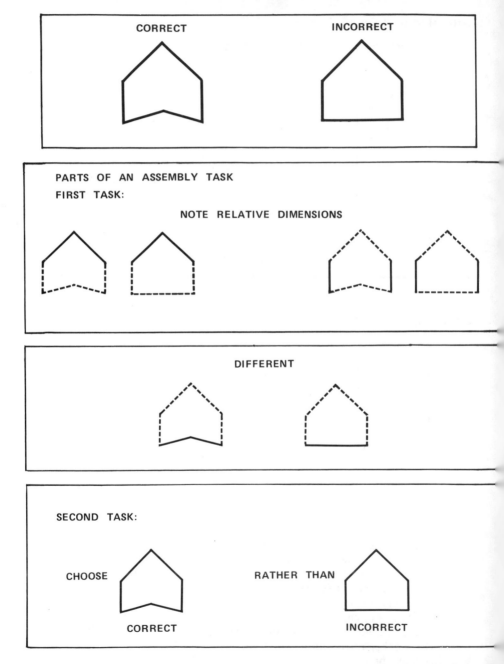

Zeaman & House (1963) were primarily interested in basic research, testing theories of discrimination learning and retardation. Gold and his associates (1971) have applied this theory and related principles and procedures in training retarded workers to master industrial tasks which had been previously considered by employers to be too complex for such employees. Gold and Scott have outlined their procedures used in job training. The reader is encouraged to study that material. Discussion of some of the same (and similar) principles is presented below.

Grouping:

Vocational trainers can group objects or stimuli in a manner which simplifies the task. For example, a list of items which belong to the same category are more easily learned than a list of words from different categories:

SIMILAR CATEGORY	DIFFERENT CATEGORIES
TRUCK	HOUSE
AUTOMOBILE	TRUCK
TRACTOR	BEET
BUS	DRESS

Breaking Down Task into Easy Stages:

It is easier to learn a difficult discrimination job task if the learning sequence begins with a fairly easy task and proceeds gradually to the more difficult task, or if sub-sections are put together first and those sub-sections then combined. (Consistent with Principles XI and XIII above, one may wish to demonstrate the entire procedure to the student several times before beginning to teach sub-components of the task and one would also end the teaching with demonstrating and having the student perform the entire task or sequence of tasks after sub-sections are learned.) See Figure V-3.

Provision of Facilitating Cues

When a learner already can make certain discriminations (for example, between colors) this skill can be used to aid the individual learn new discriminations. For example, if the task is to learn to select a hexagonal bolt rather than a pentagonal one, the initial discrimination might be made easier by painting the outside edges of hexagonal bolts with red paint, leaving the pentagonal bolts natural. When the worker learns to select "the bolt with the red outline," then hexagons with only one of the six edges painted with red can be substituted. Gradually, with new sets of bolts, the amount of paint can be reduced in length and intensity, providing the worker with more limited cues. Such procedures often facilitate learning. In a few cases, the color cue could be distracting. In such cases, some different type of cue, such as using hexagons larger than the pentagons for initial discrimination learning, and very gradually reducing difference in sizes in successive stages of training for discrimination could be employed.

FIGURE V-3

Task: To Learn to Select Specific Parts to be Fitted
Together to Make a Whole

PARTS

TO BE FITTED
TOGETHER:

AS VIEWED BY WORKER IN BOXES

SUB ASSEMBLIES:

COMPLETED ASSEMBLY

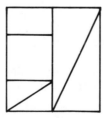

Success Striving Versus Failure Avoiding

In their early life at home and later at school, handicapped persons often experience repeated failure because the environment in which they live is designed for "normal" persons who have sensory, cognitive, or motor abilities not available to the handicapped. Cromwell and his co-workers (1963) have identified groups of individuals whom they designate "Failure Avoiders" and "Success Strivers." Such individuals seem to differ in several personality traits such as locus of control and would be expected to differ in job performance. If one is seeking for success, then he would willingly tackle new jobs, continue to try difficult tasks, and set goals above present level of performance.

A "Failure Avoider" would tend to give up easily, reject new and untried tasks, and perhaps set inappropriately low goals for himself. In general, it can be predicted that Success Strivers who are in work settings where tasks are within their physical, cognitive, and sensory capacities, would be preferable to those who are Failure Avoiders. One technique for decreasing the tendency toward "Failure Avoidance" is to initially provide the worker with tasks that are short and well within his level of competence (or below his ability level), thus insuring repeated success. It is also helpful to reduce as much as possible the potentially punishing effect of the Supervisor's "Wrong" or of failures that the worker can clearly recognize for himself.

A Note on Training Methods

Gold & Scott (1971) suggest several training methods which are helpful in teaching retarded workers discrimination job tasks. Most of these methods are well known to classroom teachers and job trainers. One Gold & Scott technique that is particularly useful is the technique of having the worker learn by matching to sample. See Figure V-4.

FIGURE V-4

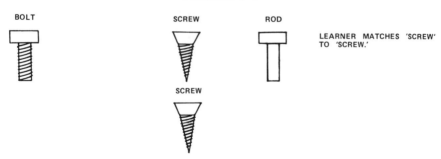

BOLT SCREW ROD

LEARNER MATCHES 'SCREW' TO 'SCREW.'

SCREW

A RELATED METHOD CONSISTS OF HAVING THE WORKER PICK OUT THE ITEM WHICH IS DIFFERENT FROM THE OTHERS OF A GROUP.

BOLT BOLT SCREW BOLT

LEARNER POINTS TO OR PICKS OUT THE ITEM WHICH IS DIFFERENT.

An important procedure in teaching work tasks to any employee, handicapped or not, is task analysis, a process whereby behavioral requirements of a specific job are identified and broken down into smaller, component parts. There is a considerable body of literature in industrial and vocational education and in psychology on this topic. Two recent texts contain excellent chapters on task analysis, one concerned with training retarded persons (Brolin, 1975) and one on organizing the curriculum in career education (Kenneke, Nystrom and Stadt, 1973).

Important to training is the analysis of tasks to be learned and determining, where relevant, the sequence of task learning. This consists of putting the component parts of a job to be learned into logical order or steps.

Teaching Complex Tasks

Below is a brief discussion of three applications of the principles derived from research on learning to the teaching of relatively complex tasks to handicapped workers.

Bicycle Brakes

Most of the persons in the post-World War II generation are familiar with the old "coaster brake" assembly on balloon tire bicycles. Persons of more recent vintage are probably more familiar with the caliper brake assemblies on the new ten speed bicycles. Both of these engineering marvels are designed to stop a moving bicycle by pressure or friction. Both must be assembled from a number of parts by an assembly line specialist or a repair man.

Gold (1972) taught a group of moderately and severely retarded adults in four different sheltered workshops to assemble both a 15-piece and a 23-piece bicycle brake (coaster and caliper brake assemblies). He used many of the established principles of learning (such as task analysis, form and color coding) to facilitate learning. His procedures are good illustrations of the potential for applying findings from research to training for the world of work.

A major point is that almost all the retarded workers of this study learned to assemble the brakes, although (according to Gold) none of the workshop directors expected any of the clients to learn the tasks at all. In fact, those who have worked in institutions for the retarded are well aware that such persons can learn complex tasks if teachers are clever.

Nuts and Bolts

Recently the authors visited a sheltered workshop with retarded workers not unlike those described in Gold's study (1972). A group of the retarded workers were seated at a bench and were charged with the task of sorting bolts of different sizes. After several moments of observation, it soon became apparent to us that the "supervisors" were doing most of the sorting. The most frequent teacher comment was "Johnny can't do it." Perhaps "Johnny" can do it. Gold and Barclay (1973), using an "easy-to-hard" training procedure, taught severely and moderately retarded workers to sort piles of bolts which were identical except for a one-eighth difference in length; these workers learned the tasks without the use of jigs.

Printed Circuit Boards

We live in a world dominated by "electronics." From radios to television to computers, our technological society has become dependent upon various electronic marvels. Behind many of these devices is an assembly called a printed circuit board. A visit to a typical assembly line will reveal a long line of workers "discriminating" between various color coded parts as they assemble the boards for later insertion in the finished product.

In the early sixties, Tate & Baroff (1967) built a workshop in which retarded and delinquent youths assembled very complex electronic equipment. Some deaf and physically handicapped persons work in TV and computer factories and on assembly lines producing fire alarm devices for homes. Gold (1973) reports that a group of moderately and severely retarded workers learned to assemble an electronic printed circuit board, using such principles as "easy-to-hard sequencing," matching to sample, and fading. Findings in this study with simple printed circuits are consistent with the Tate and Baroff study in which the workers learned to produce a complex electromechanical product (Tate & Baroff, 1967). Such activities are frequently found in workshops for handicapped persons today and many handicapped workers perform such jobs in competitive industry.

FIGURE V-5

FIGURE V-6

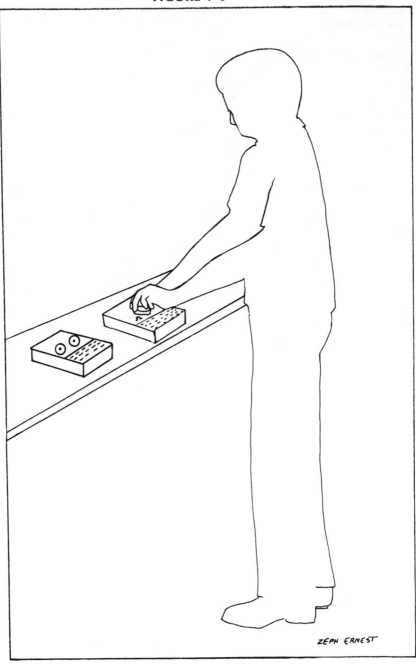

Summary

In this chapter we have selected principles and data from research studies to illustrate the *potential* that emerging educational technology offers for the vocational training of persons with disabilities. The current emphasis on comprehensive career training, spurred by the career education movement, can accelerate the process of developing new and more efficient methods for training handicapped workers to perform jobs more effectively. In doing so, perhaps their adjustment to and contribution to society may become more meaningful both to the disabled worker and co-workers.

REFERENCES

Brolin, Donn. *Vocational preparation of retarded citizens.* New York: Merrill, 1976.

Bruner, J.S. *Toward a theory of instruction.* Cambridge: Harvard University Press, 1966.

Clarke, A.B.D. Research in mental retardation and applications of research. Address presented at Fourth Conference of International Society for the Scientific Study of Mental Deficiency, Washington, D.C.: August, 1976.

Cromwell, R.L. A social learning theory approach to mental retardation. In: N.R. Ellis (Ed.) *Handbook of mental deficiency.* New York: McGraw Hill Book Co., Inc. 1963.

Crossen, J.E. A technique for programming sheltered workshop environments for training severely retarded workers. *American Journal of Mental Deficiency,* 1969, 73, 814-818.

Gardner, D.C. and Warren, S.A. Teachers' knowledge of the relationship between reading and work. *Illinois Career Education Journal,* 1977, 32 (1), 57-62.

Gold, M. Stimulus factors in skill training of the retarded on a complex assembly task: acquisition, transfer and retention. *American Journal of Mental Deficiency,* 1972, 76, 517-526.

Gold M.W. and Barclay, C.R. The learning of difficult visual discrimination by the moderately and severely retarded. *Mental Retardation,* 1973, 11, 9-11.

Gold, M.W. and Scott, K.G. Discrimination learning. In: W.B. Stephens (Ed) *Training the developmentally young.* New York: The John Day Company, 1971.

Gold M.W. *Printed circuit board assembly training for the moderately and severely retarded.* Paper presented at the 97th Annual Meeting of the American Association on Mental Deficiency, Atlanta, Georgia, May 29, 1973.

James, W. *Talks to teachers on psychology: and to students on some of life's ideals.* New York: Henry Holt & Co., 1899.

Kenneke, L.J., Nystrom, D.C. and Stadt, R.W. *Planning and organizing career curricula.* New York: Howard W. Sams & Co., Inc. 1973.

Tate, B.G. and Baroff, G.S. Training the mentally retarded in the production of a complex product. *Exceptional Children,* 1967, 33, 405-408.

Thorndike, E.L. *Animal intelligence.* New York: MacMilan, 1911.

Thorndike, E.L. *The fundamentals of learning.* New York: Columbia University, Teachers College, 1932.

Zeaman, D. and House, B. The role of attention in retardate discrimination learning. In: N.R. Ellis (Ed) *Handbook of Mental Deficiency.* New York: McGraw-Hill, 1963, 159-223.

Chapter VI

Social Learning and General Work Skills

The gap between what the educational investigator is discovering and the application of his or her findings in the classroom, shop, or work setting is well documented. This gap can be attributed in part to a "communication gap". Fortunately, two professional organizations have recently made an attempt to bridge this gap.

The American Vocational Education Research Association, an affiliate of the American Vocational Association, has recently made available a microfiche quarterly, *Journal of Vocational Education Research.* The National Association of Career Education has published a new journal which is primarily concerned with bridging this gap for the classroom teacher, *Career Education Quarterly.*

This chapter and the following chapter are written with the problem of information, dissemination, and use in mind. The reader can use these approaches as models for applying research and theory to the world of work, both in the classroom, and on the job. These two chapters are directed to teachers and practitioners to illustrate the importance of, and the *practicality of,* applying research findings, based on results of studies to the teaching of general work skills and specific job skills.

In this chapter, we propose a process for identifying critical area(s) for instructional intervention in career education and for developing instructional programs for the critical area by applying learning theory and accompanying research to instructional design. We have chosen, for purposes of illustration, psychosocial domains of career education. We will suggest techniques for applying both Rotter's Social Learning Theory (1954, 1966, 1975) and Bandura's Social Learning Theory (1974) to career education instruction in the affective domain. These will be illustrated with sample lesson plans.

In the last chapter, examples of how techniques of research in discrimination learning theory have been successfully applied to the teaching of actual work tasks to trainable retarded adolescents and adults on-the-job were described.

In the next chapter, we have included a discussion of some very interesting research in which the rate of work production (the number of pieces or tasks completed) has been significantly improved by applying social learning theory on the production line.

We have arbitrarily selected the examples and illustrations for this chapter and the succeeding chapter from a myriad of possibilities. The choice of whether or not the gap between our growing technology in education and its application in practice will diminish, is in the final analysis, one which will be made by the instructors and job trainers. Professional organizations and educational investigators have come to recognize the need for effective dissemination. The findings of educational research, and suggestions for classroom application, are increasingly available in a form that practitioners can utilize. As the saying goes, "we can lead a horse to water, but we can't make him drink". We hope that you, the reader, the classroom teacher, the practitioner, will make the appropriate choice for your students and workers.

Theoretical Base of Career Education: Rationale for Instruction

The career education movement, in part, is based on the vocational development theory of such authors as Ginzberg, Ginsberg, Axelrod, Herma, (1951), Holland (1966), and Super (1953). These theorists, and others, generally agree that vocational development (personality development as related to the world of work) is a life-long process which begins in early childhood. Thus, the multi-stage, USOE Career Education Model (see Chapter One) reflects this theoretical base. Moreover, the Kindergarten-Life (K-Life) aspect of career education is clearly stated as one of the 25 USOE major programmatic assumptions of career education:

> 5. Career development, as part of human development, begins in the preschool years, and continues into the retirement years...(Hoyt, 1975, p.6).

The acceptance of the developmental theories of career development logically leads educators to accept the notion that most individuals can learn job-hunting skills, career decision-making skills, and all the other basic world of work skills, which, when combined, can enhance the career development process for each individual (see Hoyt, 1975, p. 7).

The acceptance of the assumption that not only is career development a life-long process, but that it is based on *learned behavior* leads to the core of career education movement's rationale: that is, the assumption that educational intervention can positively affect the individual student's career development. In other words, career educators assume that such "...skills can be taught to and learned by almost everyone. (Hoyt, 1975, p. 7).

Developing Instructional Programs in Career Education to Meet Critical Needs

Most educators would agree that the assumptions stated in the previous paragraph are proper and acceptable. Professional differences and discussions would be concerned with developing answers to the next two logical questions:

1. What are the critical areas, both topics and stages, for educational intervention?

2. What are the best methods/strategies for such intervention?

It is not the intent of this section of the book to deal with all the possible answers to these questions. Instead, this section will *illustrate a process* which educators can use for developing career education instructional programs. This process will be illustrated by identifying one critical area for instruction and then presenting a proposed, general intervention plan for instruction which is based on results of learning studies. Figure VI-1 delineates the process.

FIGURE VI-1

Steps in Developing Career Education
Instructional Program

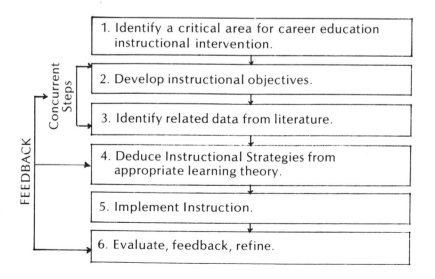

ILLUSTRATION: Social Learning Theory: Work Attitudes

1. Identifying a Critical Area

The process of identifying a critical area for career education instructional intervention should involve an extensive review of both older well established studies, current literature and the collection of data from such primary sources as parents, teachers, counselors, and other appropriate resources. An excellent starting point in the search for critical areas for career education instruction intervention is the USOE policy paper on career education, entitled *An Introduction to Career Education* (1975). In this handbook, Kenneth Hoyt, the Director of the United States Office of Career Education, outlines 25 Programmatic Assumptions of Career Education. A recent study by Gardner and Carmody (1976) suggests that special educators have often ignored the 25 basic assumptions of career education in their doctoral research.

It is generally accepted by professional educators, psychologists, and employers that one of the most critical areas in the career development process, that is, the factors which spell the difference between "success" or "failure" in the world of work, are personality factors, or the affective domain (Gardner, in press). By affective career education, we mean that portion of the career development-career education process which is concerned with helping children and adults develop appropriate attitudes, values, interests, and goals about work.

Reviews of literature in career education indicate that nearly every career education text recognized the need for "affective career education" (e.g., Bailey & Stadt, 1973, ; Wernick, 1973). Furthermore, the USOE policy paper has clearly identified this area as an important one in the Programmatic Assumptions of Career Education section (No. 23):

> 23. Good work habits and positive attitudes toward work can be taught effectively to most individuals. Assimilation of such knowledge is most effective if begun in the early childhood years. (Hoyt, 1975, p. 7).

We agree with Hoyt. For over three decades, psychologists have known that it is possible to teach cooperative behavior to rats, so surely most humans can be taught such behavior.

2. Developing Instructional Objectives

The first step in developing an instructional program in any domain is to develop meaningful and measurable objectives (Mager & Beach, 1967). It is not the intent of this section to demonstrate how one develops such instructional objectives in affective career education. Rather, we intend to illustrate ways in which one can identify and apply an appropriate learning theory to the planning of instructional strategies to meet such goals, in this case, objectives in the affective domain of career education.

The reader is referred to Mager & Beach (1967), Mager (1962), Bloom, et al (1956) and Krathwohl et al (1964) for general reference on writing instructional objectives. For specific affective career and vocational education objectives, the reader is referred to Bailey & Stadt (1973) and Porreca & Stallard (1975). Basically, the scheme for developing objectives follows a procedure of first determining terminal objectives, and then followed with specific and enabling objectives.

Sample Objectives

For purposes of illustration, we have chosen to deal with those psychosocial career education objectives which are concerned with developing cooperative work behaviors and behaviors which indicate acceptance of responsibility for one's own work. Specific Terminal objectives for these illustrative areas were taken from a recent report of common affective domain career-vocational education competencies conducted by Porreca and Stallard (1975). In this study of 111 common affective domain competencies of students in 5 vocational-technical occupations, the authors reported that at least 80% of a sample of employees (N = 40), employers (N = 51) and vocational-technical teachers (N = 100) considered 95% of the 111 affective domain competencies as important. In another section of the same report, 48 State Directors of Vocational Education were found to be in agreement on these same items. From this report, we have selected 10 cooperative behavior competencies and 10 responsible behavior competencies which were rated as highly important by the majority of the state directors in the Porreca & Stallard study.

These objectives are shown below in Tables 1 and 2. Note that these items were arbitrarily selected for purposes of illustration by the authors from a list of 91 related competencies for vocational education students which were rated important (a score of 5 or 6) on a scale of 1-6 by the 48 vocational directors surveyed. The wording of some of the competencies has been slightly modified for this illustration. The categories "Cooperative Behaviors" and "Responsible Behaviors" are our own.

TABLE VI-1
Sample Instructional Objectives for Affective
Career Education: Responsible Behaviors

---

1. Generates work independently without constant supervision.
2. Possesses a sense of responsibility for providing service.
3. Assumes responsibility for the property and safety of customers, fellow employers, and employer.*
4. Accepts responsibility to set his occupational goals.
5. Practices a self-evaluation of interests for occupational opportunities.
6. Assumes responsibility for acquiring work supplies needed in the production of goods and services.
7. Assumes responsibility for giving out or sending out information when needed.
8. Assumes responsibility for listening to the planning of work.
9. Displays systematic planning to determine a course of action.
10. Appraises quality of own work with objectivity.*

Notes:

1. From: Porreca & Stollard, 1975, 15-25.
2. Item asterisked (*) have been modified by additions or synonyms.
3. The category "Responsible Behaviors" was selected by the authors of this text. It refers to those behaviorial competencies which infer that an individual accepts responsibility for the outcomes of his or her own work behavior.

TABLE VI-2

Sample Instructional Objectives for Affective Career Education: Cooperative Behaviors

1. Displays personal satisfaction in creating a favorable image with prospective customers, employer, and fellow employees.*
2. Provides assistance to people.
3. Listens with alertness to customers' and co-workers' conversations.
4. Cooperates in requesting, giving, receiving, or discussing information in the work environment.
5. Works congenially with other people.
6. Derives satisfaction when working with others as a cooperative member of a group.
7. Enjoys cooperating with others in the work that needs to be performed.
8. Voluntarily assists other workers.*
9. Participates actively in organizing constructive work activities.
10. Develops the ability to plan and work in groups.

Notes:

1. From: Porreca & Stollard, 1975, 15-25.
2. Items asterisked (*) have been modified by additions or synonyms.
3. The category "Cooperative Behaviors" was selected by the authors of this text. It refers to those behavioral competencies which infer that an individual has internalized the attitudes, values, beliefs that cooperating with fellow human beings is both necessary and good, especially in work settings.

So far, we have identified a critical area for the development of instructional strategies in two areas considered important for career education. We have selected the general categories of "Responsible Behaviors" and "Cooperative Behaviors" (defined and illustrated in Tables VI-1 and VI-2 as areas for discussion of a process for developing instructional strategies using appropriate learning theories. We have also provided, in Tables VI-1 and VI-2, illustrative instructional objectives.

The next steps are to (1) identify (select) and describe appropriate learning theories from which to deduce instructional strategies for each category, (2) describe and define the theory and related research, and (3) describe the development of instructional techniques from the appropriate theory. (Note that the reader may prefer to operate from some different theory and can develop a similar scheme based on that theory.)

Section 3a, below, describes one appropriate theory for developing instructional strategies for "responsible behaviors" and briefly discusses related research. Section 4a describes the proposed application of this theory and related research to the design of instruction.

Sections 3b and 4b follow similar patterns in identifying, describing, and applying an appropriate learning theory to the teaching of "cooperative behaviors".

3a. Identifying a theory for developing instructional strategies for teaching "responsible behaviors" in the world of work

A review of the literature related to "accepting responsibility for one's own actions" revealed a number of related concepts or constructs such as Aronfreed's "internalized control" (1968), Crandall et al's "feeling of achievement responsibility (1962), Rotter's "internal-external locus of control" (1954, 1966, 1975).

The authors found the most clear, concise, and comprehensive explanation of this phenomena to be the social learning theory of J. B. Rotter (1954, 1966, 1975). Rotter's theory has been broadly studied since 1954 (Lefcourt, 1972). The theory continues to be an exceptionally popular area for investigation by psychologists and educators and Rotter has recently revised the theory and clarified areas of misconceptions based on extensive recent research (1975).

One major concept of the Rotter theory is locus of control. Simply stated, locus of control refers to the degree to which an individual, person (e.g., student, worker) accepts responsibility for the outcomes of his or her own behavior. A person who believes that what happens to him is a result of his own behavior is said to have an "internal locus of control". Conversely, a person who believes that what happens to him is a matter of "luck," "chance," or the whims of "powerful others" is said to have an "external locus of control".

What this means in the context of the world of work is that persons who are more "internal" will probably achieve more (work harder) than those who are external. There is considerable research evidence to support this notion (see reviews by Joe (1971), Lefcourt (1966, 1972).)

Moreover, two recent studies have indicated a significant relationship between locus of control and career maturity in women (Gable, 1973) and in ninth graders (Thomas, 1974). The implications from these studies are that persons with internal locus of control are more mature "career-wise" than those who are external.

The next questions we asked in our review of the literature were (1) can a person's locus of control be changed through instructional programs? and (2) what are the implications for the disabled?

In terms of changing or modifying a person's locus of control, Mac-Donald (1972) has reviewed several studies which indicate that a person's locus of control can be modified from external to more internal, e.g. a worker can be taught to accept responsibility for "quality of his own work". The outlook for successful intervention here seems promising.

From the point of view of the disabled, the modification of external approaches to work seems critical. Several reviews of the literature (Gardner, 1974; Lawrence & Winschel, 1975) concluded that persons with disabilities tend *to be more external* than their normal peers. The findings in a recent study by Gardner, Warren & Gardner (1977) are consistent with the previous research.

If, then, persons with disabilities are more external in locus of control and locus of control is modifiable through instruction, then our next step is to design instructional programs which will help disabled persons become more accepting of responsibility for their own behaviors, including behaviors at work.

4a. Developing Responsible Behaviors: Applying Rotter's Theory to the Instructional Program

In a recent article, Gardner & Gardner (1973) point to the need for special class teachers to develop classroom techniques which will ensure that their pupils develop more realistic beliefs about outcomes of their own behaviors. The problem, in the context of affective career education, is for teachers to develop instructional strategies which will help pupils to see the relationship between their own behaviors at work (or in school) and the resulting reinforcements. Figure VI-2 outlines the two-fold instructional design problem:

FIGURE VI-2
Two-fold Instructional Design Problem

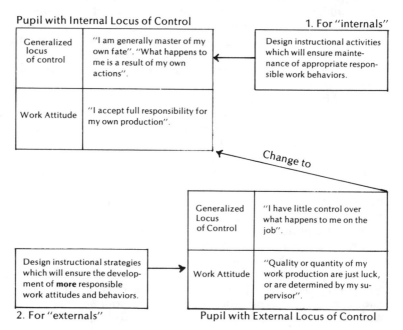

Pupil with Internal Locus of Control

1. For "internals"

| Generalized locus of control | "I am generally master of my own fate". "What happens to me is a result of my own actions". |
| Work Attitude | "I accept full responsibility for my own production". |

Design instructional activities which will ensure maintenance of appropriate responsible work behaviors.

Change to

| Generalized Locus of Control | "I have little control over what happens to me on the job". |
| Work Attitude | "Quality or quantity of my work production are just luck, or are determined by my supervisor". |

Design instructional strategies which will ensure the development of **more** responsible work attitudes and behaviors.

2. For "externals"   Pupil with External Locus of Control

Goals for those who already tend to be "internal" are to maintain responsible attitudes whereas goals for those who tend to be "external" are to develop more feelings of their own responsibility by outcomes, and then maintain those feelings.

A SAMPLE LESSON PLAN*

The lesson plan below is based on certain assumptions. These assumptions are derived from current theory and research on locus of control and children with special needs.

1. Students with disabilities (special needs), as a group, tend to be more external in locus of control than their normal peers. This factor is very important to the teaching of work behaviors and is related to career maturity.

2. An individual's locus of control can be changed from external to internal through involvement in an educational program which is designed to teach a person to see the relationship between his or her own behavior and the reinforcements he or she receives.

We have selected, for illustration, item number 10 from Table 1, page 87, as the instructional objective for this lesson.

SAMPLE LESSON PLAN #1

AREA: Responsible Behavior: #10, Appraises quality of own work with objectivity
Subject: Job Preparation
Age range of students: 16-21
Time Alloted: Approximately 50 minutes
Number of students in class: 12

OVERALL OBJECTIVE: Student will be able to identify those aspects of the task which are crucial to adequate performance of the task and judge his own work to determine the degree to which his work is acceptable.

TASK FOR THIS LESSON: Labeling envelopes, folding pages to be inserted, and inserting folded pages into envelopes.

SPECIFIC OBJECTIVES FOR THIS LESSON:

Student will:
1. Learn to follow a sequence of steps in performing the total task.
2. Learn the procedures for performing each part of the total series of steps required for completing the total task.
3. Be able to identify the important and relevant parts of the completed task, such as appropriate placement of label, folding into three approximately equal horizontal segments, placing all envelopes face

*(Described here in greater detail than a teacher would write into plan book in order to make illustration clearer to reader)

down, with open end in same direction (for machine sealing), placing into a large box.

ENABLING OBJECTIVES:

Student will:

1. Learn the "correct" placement of labels, i.e., on envelope with the flap away from worker when placement is made.
2. Place labels on envelope with written materials (names and addresses) placed right side up for reading.
3. Fold pages into approximately three equal parts, horizontal folding.
4. Place completed envelopes together, all with flaps facing in consistent direction, in a large box.
5. Learn the steps 1 through 4 above well enough to check their own work against the models for the steps that are furnished for them.
6. Identify those parts of the job that were done incorrectly and correct their own mistakes.

MATERIALS:

Chalkboard
240 envelopes, long business style (#10)
240 stickers with names and addresses on them
240 sheets of paper, mimeographed with information (e.g., letters)
2 cardboard boxes (e.g., food can size), open top
Tables or desks for working
Models for comparison:

(1) Envelope with label attached, pasted on cardboard (about 8½ by 11 inches), with flap open and extending above top of envelope to indicate the correct placement of label.
(2) Sheet of paper of type to be inserted in envelope, pasted on similar cardboard with center portion pasted flat against the cardboard, top and bottom left free.
(3) One completed envelope with paper inserted, pasted with label against cardboard and flap open at top, entire envelope including top pasted flat.

MOTIVATION: These students are aware of the value of money and of jobs; they already know that jobs are not paid for (or jobs are lost) if work is unsatisfactory to employer or contractor. The motivation will therefore be inherent after a brief explanation to them that one of the important aspects of work and keeping a job, as well as of amount paid for piece work, is the ability to check one's work for accuracy and quality.

PROCEDURE:

1. Brief discussion with group of importance of being able to appraise one's own work, with teacher asking leading questions or making explanations as needed.
2. Put models on display in place where all students can see them.
3. Demonstrate entire process once to students.

4. Demonstrate the folding aspect, calling attention to importance of folding (with the folds being at approximately equal distance from ends of pages, but with the two ends being slightly smaller than the center section).
5. Give each student a letter to fold. On completion, the student is to take his work to the sample model, compare it and decide whether it "matches." Teacher will be near sample when student checks and student will tell teacher if his work matches sample. If not, why not? What should be done to achieve match? Student goes to pile of letters, takes another one, and tries again. Repeat until student is accurate and knows the parts of the task that are most likely to cause difficulty (for that individual student). (This can be done by students working individually within a group and discussing informally the problems that arise in folding "correctly.")
6. When all students have learned folding task, teacher demonstrates again the envelope stuffing, with the letter placed into the envelope in such a way that the part closest to the opening being the fold and the top of letter being at top of opening. (To ensure that when flap is opened later, the letter will be opened ready for reading instead of the reader seeing signature first.)
7. Each student gets envelope and stuffs it. (N.B. If at this stage there is a student who still cannot fold properly, that student may watch the insertion demonstration and return to task of folding; teacher may need to demonstrate individually to that student when he is ready for inserting letters.)
8. Each student takes his stuffed envelope to the sample on cardboard and checks it against that model. Teacher is nearby to ensure that student checks properly, to help student identify errors and discuss ways of correcting. If needed, have students repeat insertions. (They can use the same folded letters, simply removing them, opening folds, re-folding, and re-inserting.) Those students who learn the folding and insertion task can then begin working on the task placing stuffed envelopes in a box large enough for them to lie loosely (e.g., canned foods box).
9. When all students have learned to insert, class is brought together as a group again and teacher demonstrates manner of laying stuffed envelope flat on table, flap open and facing away from student, checking to be sure label is right side up, and placing label on envelope in "correct" place.
10. Student tries one, checks it, as in above steps. As students each learn to identify potential problems and correct them, they may begin to place labels on the envelopes that are already stuffed and in box. As they finish the first few, each should be checked against the model because this is one of the more difficult parts of the task. When teacher has "checked out for independent work" of each student, that student may begin to label stuffed envelopes. THROUGHOUT THIS ACTIVITY AND OTHER INDEPENDENTLY DONE PARTS, STRONG EMPHASIS

SHOULD BE PLACED ON CHECKING AGAINST THE MODEL FREQUENTLY, WATCHING STUFFED ENVE-LOPES FOR ERRONEOUSLY STUFFED ONES WHICH SHOULD BE PLACED ASIDE, AND ON *QUALITY* OF WORK RATHER THAN QUANTITY.

11. When all the envelopes are stuffed there will be less than 240 because some letters, labels or envelopes have been spoiled. All spoiled items will have been placed in the "reject" box. Teacher will call class together. Discuss items in reject box, with *effort to avoid having students assign errors to other students,* but allowing students to admit their own early mistakes and laugh at them if they choose to do so. The types of errors made, ways of avoiding them, and problems can be discussed. Sample questions:

    Why are the edges of this letter not in line?

    Where will the stamp be placed on this upside-down-labeled envelope?

    Can one make mistakes even after he has learned a job and if so, what might cause this? (Tiredness, inattention, talking to neighbor, etc.)

    What is the advantage of having all flaps left open? (Machine sealing and stamping)

    After the discussion, each student is given 9 (or proportionate number available) stuffed, labeled envelopes to check. If an error is found, the student is to place in reject box. Then the student passes his checked batch to a second student for double checking.

12. Final discussion of the task, based on errors found in the student checking, with Teacher spot checking during discussion.

13. Rejects are thrown away, without comment but clearly indicating that they are worthless. Then, all envelopes are placed in same position, flaps open, in box, Teacher with students doing a third general check as placements are made.

3b. Identifying a theory for developing instructional strategies for teaching "cooperative behaviors" in the world of work

Since social learning theory, in a generic sense, is concerned with how people learn from people, social situations, and interactions with others, the review of literature for this section focused on social learning theories. Rotter's theory, of course, clearly has application to the teaching of cooperative behaviors, especially those objectives which relate to learning to accept responsibility for team or group efforts on the job.

Another well-developed, well-supported theory which can be used for illustration of theoretical application to teaching strategies for cooperative learning is Bandura's social learning theory (1977). This theory is sometimes called Modeling or Imitation Theory. In laymen's terms, it is referred to as the "monkey-see, monkey-do" theory, perhaps because some of the early research on modeling was done with monkeys.

Instructors who use this theory in their work can expect their pupils to exhibit:

...rapid acquisition of complex behaviors, particularly affective behaviors...(and will soon discover that)...many learnings can be taught to relatively passive learners, a situation similar to the typical classroom situation (MacDonald, 1970, p. 100).

Moreover, in an extensive study of improving work performance of retarded adolescents, Kliebhan (1967) found "modeling techniques" significantly more effective than other approaches. (This study will be reviewed in the next chapter.)

Simply stated, modeling theory attempts to explain how people learn, through observation of other people. This theory is based on the premise that *PEOPLE CAN LEARN BY EXAMPLE*. Modeling is particularly successful if the person that an individual learner or worker is observing (learning from) is a "significant" person. A significant person is an important person from the learner's point of view. These important persons are often referred to as "models" or "role models". Bandura (1977) uses the term "modeling" to refer to these phenomena, in social learning theory, which are subsumed under the labels "identification" and "imitation". According to Bandura, modeling can produce at least three effects. These effects are important to the designing of instructional programs.

1. ACQUIRE NEW LEARNINGS: Students who observe others can acquire new patterns of behaviors by watching these significant person(s) perform.

2. STRENGTHEN OR WEAKEN PREVIOUS LEARNINGS: Students can weaken (inhibit) or strengthen previously learned responses by watching others. This is particularly true when the observer watches the model(s) receive rewards (or punishments) for his or her behavior.

3. ELICIT CUED RESPONSES: A student observing the behavior of another may use this behavior as a *cue* for performing previously learned behaviors. For example, people will begin clapping in response to the clapping of other people.

4b. Developing Cooperative Behaviors: Applying Modeling Theory to the Instructional Program.

Simply stated, modeling theory, to be applied here, is concerned with use of the "monkey-see, monkey-do" principle to teach workers and students to get along with each other, to cooperate with their fellow workers, in group or team efforts aimed at completing work tasks.

In applying modeling theory to the teaching of cooperative work behaviors, the teacher should make each lesson plan accountable for meeting the optimum learning conditions of the four subprocesses outlined in Bandura's theory. These processes are delineated in the lesson plan checksheet in figure 3.

FIGURE VI-3

Lesson Plan Checksheet
Teaching Cooperative Work Behaviors

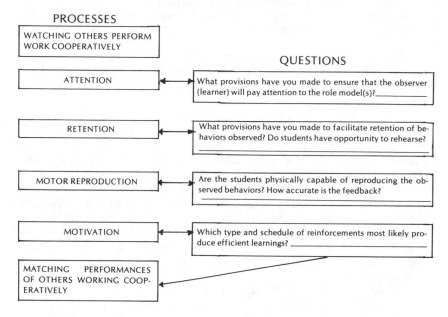

The lesson plan below is based on the following assumptions deduced from modeling theory and related research.

1. Students with special needs can learn effectively, just as other students can, by observing and matching the performances of other significant persons, on the job, or in the classroom. Some students who have communication problems (e.g., deaf, retarded) may learn more effectively through modeling than by verbal instruction.

2. Students and workers can learn appropriate work attitudes as they relate to, or are inferred by, cooperative work behaviors, by observing and matching the work performance of their peers or other role models (who have already acquired such appropriate behaviors) while participating in group or team projects.

3. Students or workers who have acquired the appropriate work behaviors previously, will have these learnings reinforced (strengthened) by participating in such group events.

4. The inappropriate, previously learned, uncooperative behaviors, will be inhibited (weakened) in these students who are learning "new", appropriate cooperative behaviors by observing and matching the appropriate behaviors of their peers.

A SAMPLE LESSON PLAN

AREA: Cooperative Behaviors: #8 Voluntarily assists other workers
   Subject: Job Preparation

Age Range: 16 to 21
Time Allotted: About 30 minutes
Number of Students in Class: 12

OVERALL OBJECTIVE: Students will recognize when another student is in need of help and volunteer to help if appropriate.

TASK FOR THIS LESSON: Playing the Bottle game.

SPECIFIC OBJECTIVES FOR THIS LESSON:
1. To help students see clearly that this society is one in which citizens are interdependent to some extent and thus cooperation can facilitate activity.
2. To help students recognize that others can be helpful.
3. To help individual students recognize that each has something to offer to others at some time and that one can attain personal recognition for it.
4. To help students recognize that working together can sometimes result in everybody getting something and that excessive competition can result in all but one losing, or even in "everybody loses."

N.B.: This is only one of many activities that would be used to try to teach cooperative behavior. It is often highly effective to teach this behavior in the context of some other lesson. Unless students are given a large variety of experience in cooperative behavior, they may not transfer what is learned in one situation to another, especially if the students are socially not very perceptive.

ENABLING OBJECTIVES:
Students will:
1. Be able to identify specific problems that arise when competition is high, each individual trying to be the only winner.
2. Recognize that it can be pleasant to work together.
3. Recognize that by planning and working together, each can "be a winner."
4. Verbalize understandings of the importance of cooperation as opposed to strong competition in which one wins (maybe) and everybody else loses.

MATERIALS:
2 large bottles, e.g., quart size ginger ale bottles
1 ball of string
12   10 penny nails
Watch (Teacher's) with sweep second hand
1 package of candy (or chewing gum or other inexpensive items that these students have indicated a liking for)

MOTIVATION: The game itself has intrinsic motivation for both children and adults, as indicated by use of the procedure by one of the authors (SAW) with individuals of various ages. For the discussion, the Teacher may need to encourage students with comments, appropriate to these students; however, experience in use of the game suggests that students are quite willing to discuss results and enjoy doing so.

PROCEDURE:

Since there are 12 students, the procedure will work best if the total group is divided in half, six students to each group. Do this first, using any procedure the teacher feels appropriate. (This assumes that the teacher is sensitive to student needs and would not have a "choose up sides" approach with a group of students having disabilities).

1. Divide class into 2 groups of 6 each.
2. Tie a nail to one end of a piece of string four feet long and a piece of chalk to the other end. Use this to draw a circle with chalk on the floor in an open area.
3. Choose which group takes the first chance at playing the game. This can be done by having students all guess at a 3 digit number that Teacher has written on piece of paper and placed on desk, with group having a student guessing closest to Teacher's number being first, or cutting deck of cards, group having student getting highest card going first, or by any other chance method.
4. Tell students rules of the game. These are:
    (1) Each student makes himself a string with nail on end. Strings are four feet long (shorter if students are poorly coordinated).
    (2) Bottle is set in center of circle. Each student places his nail touching bottle and with string stretched out straight to edge of circle; this should produce a radiation of strings with each student's string being far enough from others on the circle to permit student to stand.
    (3) Object of game is to place nail in bottle without touching nail.
    (4) Only one hand may be used, the preferred hand; other hand is placed behind student's back for working.
    (5) Each student must pick up free end of his string when Teacher calls "START" and try to get his string in bottle before anyone else does. (This will require students to wad up string in one hand as they move toward bottle and nail at end, a task that requires coordination and which may result in dropping parts of string and having to recover because string is picked up. Student is required to hold it, not simply walk forward and pick up the string at any point. Teacher can demonstrate beginning of task but should not put nail in bottle.)
    (6) Teacher tells first group that the winner, (person who gets nail in first) will get a piece of candy (or other small reward).
5. First group plays game. (It will be found that as they get near bottle, some strings may entangle, some students will try to get their nail to knock another's nail off center over bottle, etc.) This group gets to play the game 3 or 4 times, with a "winner" each time. Teacher keeps time to determine how long it takes for winner to get nail in bottle.

6. Second group plans game. Rules are same, but this time Teacher tells students that each student will get a reward if all nails are in bottle within time limits, but Teacher does not tell them what the secret of time limit is. Allow second group 2 or 3 minutes to plan a strategy for playing the game.
7. Second group plays. If these students are similar to others who have played the game, it will be found that students will discuss with each other various strategies for "beating the deadline" and will call out encouraging remarks to each other; for example, if they have decided to take turns getting nail into bottle and one student is slower than expected, someone usually calls out a request for skipping ahead by a player who is ahead. Allow this group to play the game one or more times, rewarding on each game. (They may need more than one trial in order to ensure that all students get their nail in.)

DISCUSSION:

8. Teacher discusses with students as a total group results in terms of time required, problems encountered.
9. The groups play a second game. For example, this time they may have the bottle at end of room and the nails with strings placed on a line 6 feet away. At the START, each student must pick up his string by end that is away from nail and carry it to bottle, getting it in without wadding up string, but instead each player must hold string by its end and try to get nail into bottle without wadding up string. The team that gets all nails in first will win. Teams may choose to go all at once or one at a time. (If they model, they should choose to go one at a time because after the experience in the game played in circle, the group that all tried to get nail in at once should have done less well than the group that planned to take turns and this should have come in the discussion.)

N.B.: If for some unforeseen reason the group that played the game first was cooperative, there may not have been a need for the lesson.

*The authors express appreciation to Paula L. Gardner, Department of Special Education, Boston University, for helping write the lesson plans presented in this chapter.

REFERENCES

Aronfreed, J., *Conduct and conscience: the socialization of internalized control over behavior:* New York: Academic Press, 1968.

Bailey, L.T., and Stadt, Ronald, *Career education: new approaches to human development* Bloomington, Illinois: The McKnight Publishing Company, 1973.

Bandura, Albert. *Social Learning Theory.* Englewood Cliffs, New Jersey: Prentice-Hall, Inc., 1977.

Bloom, B.S., ed., Taxonomy of Educational Objectives; the classification of educational goals, by a committee of college and university examiners, New York: Longmans, Green, 1956.

Crandall, V.V., Kotkovsky, W., and Preston, A., Motivational and ability determinants of young children's intellectual achievement behaviors. *Child Development,* 1962, 36, 643-661.

Gable, R.K., Perceptions of personal control and conformity of vocational choice as correlates of vocational development. American Personnel and Guidance Association Paper, 1973, ERIC ED082086.

Gardner, D.C., Goal-setting, locus of control and work performance of mentally retarded adults, *Dissertation Abstracts International,* 1974, Volume 35, No. 2, NO. 74-17, 924.

Gardner, D.C. Research and practice in career education (Editorial), *Career Education Quarterly,* 1976, 1(1).

Gardner, D.C., A social learning theory approach to affective career education. *Career Education Digest,* In press.

Gardner, D.C. and Carmody, S., *Research trends in career education and vocational education for mentally retarded persons.* Paper presented at New England Educational Research Organization, Convention, Provincetown, Mass.: May 1, 1976.

Gardner, D.C., and Gardner, P.L., Locus of control as related to learning effectiveness, Reading Improvement, 1974 11(2) 41-42.

Gardner, D.C., Warren, S.A. and Gardner, P.L., Locus of control and law knowledge: a comparison of normal, retarded and learning disabled adolescents, *Adolescence,* 1977, 12 (45), 103-109.

Ginzberg, E., Ginsberg, S.W., Axelrod, S., and Herma, J.R., *Occupational choice: an approach to a general theory,* New York: Columbia University Press, 1951.

Holland, J.L., A theory of vocational choice, *Journal of Counselling Psychology,* 1959, 6(1) 35-45.

Hoyt, K.L., *An introduction to career education: a policy paper of the U.S. office of education,* (DHEW publication No. OE 75-00504), Washington, D.C.: U.S. Government Printing Office, 1975.

Joe, V.C., Review of the internal-external control construct as a personality variable, *Psychological Reports,* 1971, 28, 619-40.

Kliebhan, J.M., Effects of goal-setting and modeling on job performance of retarded adolescents, *American Journal of Mental Deficiency,* 1967, 72, 220-26.

Krathwolh, D.R., Bloom, B.S., and Masia, B.B. *Taxonomy of educational objectives—the classification of educational goals*—Handbook II: Affective domain, New York: David McKay Company, Incorporated, 1964.

Lawrence, E.A., and Winschel, J.F., Locus of control: implications for special education, *Exceptional Children,* 1975, 44, 483-490.

Lefcourt, H.M. Internal versus external control of reinforcement: a review, *Psychological Reports,* 1966, 65, 206-20.

Lefcourt, H.M., Recent developments in the study of locus of control, in: B.A. Maher (ed.) *Progress in experimental personality research,* New York: Academic Press, 1972.

MacDonald, A.P., Jr., Internal-external locus of control change-technics, *Rehabilitation Literature,* 1972, 33, 44-47.

McDonald, F., Social learning theory and the design of instructional systems, *The Affective Domain,* Washington, D.C.: Communications Service Corporation, 1970.

Mager, R.F. *Preparing instructional objectives,* Palo Alto, California: Fearon Publishers, 1962.

Mager, R.F. and Beach, K.M., Jr., *Developing vocational instruction,* Palo Alto, California: Fearon Publishers, 1967.

Porreca, A.G., and Stallard, J.J., *Common affective domain competencies of students among vocational areas* (Final Report) Nashville, Tennessee: The Tennessee Research Coordinating Unit, University of Tennessee, College of Education, Tennessee State Board for Education, 1975, Research series No. 47.

Rotter, J.B., Generalized expectancies for internal versus external control of reinforcement, *Psychological Monographs,* 1966, 80 (1) (Whole No. 609).

Rotter, J.B., *Social learning and clinical psychology,* New York: Prentice-Hall, 1954.

Rotter, J.B., Some problems and misconceptions related to the construct of internal versus external control of reinforcement, *Journal of Consulting and Clinical Psychology,* 1975, 43. 56-57.

Super, D.E., A theory of vocational development, *American Psychologist,* 1953, 8 (4), 185-190.

Thomas, H.B., The effects of sex, occupational choice and career development responsibility on the career maturity of ninth grade students, American Educational Research Association paper, 1974, ERIC ED092819.

Wernick, W., *Teaching for career development in the elementary school: a life-centered approach,* Worthington, Ohio: Charles A. Jones Publishing Company, 1973.

Chapter VII

Goal Setting and Work Production: Narrowing the Competitive Gap

Chapter VI describes processes for identifying and applying research findings to the teaching of general work skills. For purposes of illustration of the process, we selected two learning theories and presented sample lesson plans which illustrated their application to the affective domain of career education. The process consisted of:

(1) *Identifying the critical area,* the "affective domain of career education,"

(2) *Developing instructional objectives.* Examples of instructional objectives were for "cooperative behaviors" and "responsible behaviors."

(3) *Identifying appropriate theory.* In this case, we selected Rotter's social learning theory as concerned with "locus of control" and Bandura's modeling theory.

(4) *Developing instructional strategies* based on theory.

We developed two illustrative lesson plans, one for each theory.

In this chapter we will not repeat the discussion of the previous chapter by describing how this process can be applied to discover critical areas for teaching job tasks. The process of identifying a critical area for job training, developing instructional training objectives, identifying related theories and developing training procedure is quite similar to the one outlined in the previous chapter on general work skills. The focus here will be on some examples of how learning principles have been applied successfully in the world of work. Most of the workers in these examples are mentally retarded, educable and trainable who are older adolescents or adults.

The Theory

If one begins to read the literature concerned with how people set goals, and goal-directed behavior, one is initially overwhelmed by the sheer volume of reports which have been published on the topic since the early 1930's. On the basis of the volume of attention given to the subject, one can conclude that the study of goals, goal-setting and goal-directed behavior is an important one to psychologists and educators. Clearly, there is no doubt that

> ...Goals are intimately related to learning. Learning of some kind is necessary to acquire goals. They are influential in the activity stream because of, and according to, the learning how to act so that the anticipated effects can be reached (Rethingshafer, 1963, 188-89).

There are a number of reviews of the research accomplished over two decades (1930-1950) in the study of level of aspiration (LOA). These reviews are useful for educators and job trainers who are interested in applying goal-setting procedures in the classroom or work site. Studying the reviews by Lewin et al (1944), Rotter (1942), and Ricciuti (1951) will provide the reader with a basic introduction to the field. (In this chapter, the terms "goal-setting" and "level of aspiration" are used synonymously.)

FIGURE VII-1

Typical Research Design for Studying
Goal-setting as a Dependent Variable

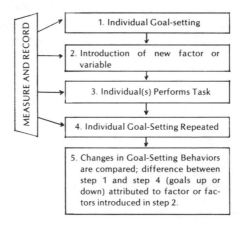

Note: In research studies, the independent variable is the one which the experimenter manipulates. The dependent variable is the one which is measured by the experimenter to determine how it varies under different conditions.

Even though the volume of studies on level of aspiration (LOA) is extensive, most investigators have not studied goal-setting as an *independent variable*. Rather, the focus of such studies has been on goal setting as a *dependent variable*. In other words, these studies have been concerned, for the most part, with what happens to a person's goal-setting behavior rather than with what happens to a person's performance if he or she sets a goal. The two basic approaches to studying goal-setting behaviors are illustrated in Figures VII-1 and VII-2.

FIGURE VII-2

Typical Research for Studying
Goal-setting as an Independent Variable

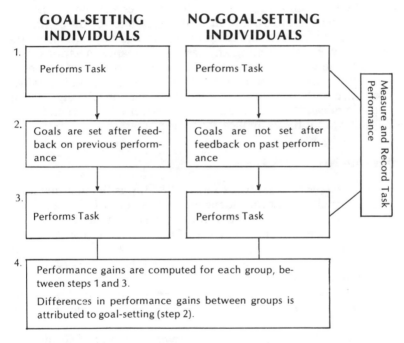

There are many variations on the two basic designs shown above in Figures VII-1 and VII-2. The first category always asks the question, "What happens to a person's goal-setting behavior when a specific factor or condition is introduced?" The other category asks, "What happens to a person's task performance after goal setting?"

In this chapter, we are concerned with those studies which have investigated goal-setting as an independent variable, particularly implications and potential for helping persons with disabilities improve their work production. Three more recent reviews of the literature on goal-setting have attended to this category and some of the studies discussed in these reviews will be described later (Fryer, 1964; Gardner, 1974; Warner & DeJung, 1969).

In recent years, the study of goals and goal-directed behavior has been facilitated by Rotter's social learning theory (1954). In Rotter's theory, goals are postulated as *important determinants of behavior*. According to Rotter's theory, Postulate 7,

> The occurrence of a behavior of a person is determined not only by the nature or importance of goals or reinforcements but also by the person's anticipation or expectancy that these goals will occur (1954, 102).

It can be hypothesized from Rotter's theory, that work production of goal-setting workers will differ in a significant way (other factors being equal) from the production of workers who do not set goals.

What happens to behavior when people set goals for themselves? What are the implications for career education, especially for the disabled? The answers to these questions will be examined below by first reviewing several studies of retarded and non-retarded populations on the relationship between goal-setting and task performance in various tasks not related to the world of work. Second, we will review two studies of non-retarded populations and two studies of retarded populations which were concerned with work task training or production. Finally, we will discuss the implications of this research for career education and make some suggestions for future application to new areas.

Studies with Non-Work Tasks

Armstrong (1947), according to Fryer (1964) was the first investigator to focus on goal-setting as an independent variable (see Figure 2). Thus, Armstrong was primarily interested in the presence or absence of goal-setting. She compared the performance of a group of normal adults on the Minnesota Rate of Manipulation Test, some of whom expressed and some who did not express goals. She found that goal-setting resulted in significantly superior performance.

Kausler (1959) found that goal-setting introductory psychology students outperformed peers who did not set goals on a 25 item arithmetic practice test.

Warner and DeJung (1969) studied the performance of 80 educable mentally retarded adolescents on a spelling task and found that those who set goals performed significantly higher than those who did not. In a more recent study, Gardner & Gardner (in press) found that a group of high school educable mentally retarded and learning disabled students assigned to a partially integrated school program significantly improved their spelling and vocabulary scores after the introduction of goal-setting procedures in the classroom.

Studies currently underway by Warren and co-workers using children with learning disabilities suggest, in preliminary analysis, that goal-setting, whether imposed or individually set, facilitates paired associate learning.

From these studies, it appears that setting goals in some types of tasks does improve performance, at least in short term studies of the phenomenon.

Application to Work Task Training and Production Task Training with Normal Intelligence Populations

Lockette, in 1956, asked a group of junior and senior high school students of normal intelligence to plane a piece of wood to preset dimensions. This is a typical shop work task on which the students had not received previous training. Students were randomly assigned to three groups: (1) students who set unrealistic goals, (2) students who set realistic goals, and (3) no-goal-setting. Each student performed the task six times. Lockette found that students who set goals, whether realistic or unrealistic, performed significantly better than students who set no goals.

In 1964, Fryer studied the effects of goal-setting on the training in the use of the International Morse Code by a large group of college freshmen and sophomores. In addition to studying goal-setting versus no-goal-setting performance outcomes, he examined several other variables not of direct concern here. With his college population, Fryer found that goal-setting students outperformed peers on difficult tasks only. The phenomenon that goal-setting apparently did not improve work performance with college students except on difficult tasks was partially substantiated in a recent study by Gardner & Warren (in press) in which no differences were found in performances between goal-setting and no-goal-setting college students on a simple clerical task.

These studies suggest that for adolescents and young adults of average or higher intelligence, the advantages of goal-setting may vary, depending on task difficulty. For a simple motor task performed by adolescents, goal-setting enhanced performance, but for the selected populations of college students, goal-setting did not affect performance on simple cognitive or clerical tasks, but did enhance complex cognitive task performance.

Increasing Work Production with Retarded Workers

In 1967, Kliebhan studied performance of forty-eight educable, mentally retarded, adolescent workers in a sheltered workshop assigned to three groups: (1) sixteen in goal-setting, (2) sixteen in imitation, and (3) sixteen control subjects. Each work crew of sixteen persons was kept intact throughout a five week period. Each work team was assigned to the shop at a different time of day so that there could be no personal communication between individuals from different groups. Each work team worked for forty-five minutes per day for the five week period. The work task consisted of affixing tapes to the pages of an unbound advertising booklet. Base rates were established prior to the experiment and daily production scores were the actual number of strips of tapes affixed each shift. The design is illustrated in Figure VII-3.

FIGURE VII-3

An Illustrated Design for
Studying Goal-setting, Imitation, and
No-goal-setting. (Kliebhan, 1967)

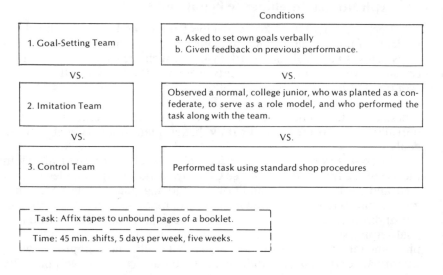

Conditions

| 1. Goal-Setting Team | a. Asked to set own goals verbally
b. Given feedback on previous performance. |

VS.   VS.

| 2. Imitation Team | Observed a normal, college junior, who was planted as a confederate, to serve as a role model, and who performed the task along with the team. |

VS.   VS.

| 3. Control Team | Performed task using standard shop procedures |

Task: Affix tapes to unbound pages of a booklet.

Time: 45 min. shifts, 5 days per week, five weeks.

For purposes of data analysis, the production scores were averaged for the week. Kliebhan found that both social learning theory-based procedures, the Imitation Team (see previous chapter) and the goal-setting group did not differ from each other in performance. However, the goal-setting group (and the imitation group) significantly outperformed the no-goal-setting, standard shop procedures control group!

In a 1974 study, Gardner matched a group of forty-eight mentally retarded adults who were employed in a workshop on the basis of past production rates and assigned them to four goal-setting and two no-goal-setting conditions at random. Workers were also matched on the basis of internal versus external locus of control test scores. Locus of control condition for this study was determined by dichotomizing the sample (internal versus external locus of control) on the basis of a median split of group scores on a slightly modified form of the Bialer Children's Locus of Control Scale (Bialer, 1961; Gardner, Warren and Gardner, 1977). The task used was a typical shop task (affixing labels to bacon packages) and each worker had performed the task for pay prior to the experiment. All workers in this study were paid the standard rate for the work performed. Initial production rates were determined by a time-study conducted one week prior to the study. All work was performed in a typical shop production room. (See Figure VII-4). It was not practical to separate the various teams during transportation time to and from work or during coffee breaks or lunch. Supervisors, however, were asked to record any conversations which might confound the design. No such conversations were reported.

Since some of the clients in the Gardner study could not read and/or had difficulty with understanding numbers, a special goal-setting procedure was designed. The measure used to determine performance was height of the stack of packages to which labels were posted. Goals were set by having the worker indicate with a wooden pointer the height of the stack expected for the next trial on a vertical "yardstick." Workers set goals or had the supervisors set them, after the supervisor had used the pointer to indicate the individual worker's performance on the previous shift. Goals were set individually just before each performance. See Figure VII-4.

An analysis of the data revealed that the locus of control variable did not seem to make a difference in production rates. The most important finding, for the purposes of this chapter, is that goal setting, regardless of locus of control or method of goal setting, was found to yield significantly better performance than no-goal-setting!

FIGURE VII-4

Production Room Layout

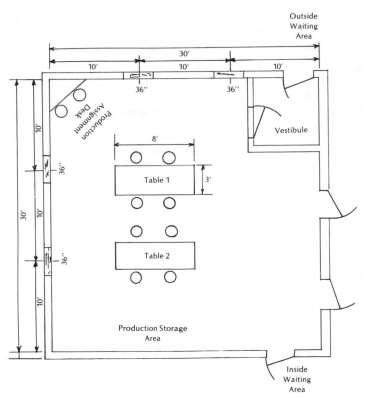

The basic design of the study is illustrated in Figure VII-5, below:

FIGURE VII-5

Illustrated Design for Studying Goal-setting Methods, No-goal-setting, Locus of Control Personality Type and Work Performance of Mentally Retarded Adults

METHOD OF GOAL SETTING			
Internal locus of control	At request of shift supervisor, each worker **sets own goals.**	Each worker is **assigned a goal** by his or her shift supervisor.	**No goal-setting.** Work performed using standard shop procedures.
External locus of control	At request of shift supervisor, each worker **sets own goals.**	Each worker is **assigned a goal** by his or her shift supervisor.	**No goal-setting.** Work performed using standard shop procedures.

Notes:

1. Time: Random assignment to one 20 minute shift for each of 6 groups, six work periods for 5 days.
2. Team assignments: Made on basis of matched random assignment for both time-study production rate and locus of control.
3. Task: Affix an adhesive backed label in a designated spot on surface of a printed cardboard bacon package, after removing label from a roll of labels.
4. Supervisor Assignments: Assigned to teams at random.
5. Feedback: All workers in all teams given feedback on past (most recent) performance prior to goal-setting/working.

These studies on one population of disabled workers, mentally retarded, generally support the findings of investigators who studied nonretarded persons and individuals doing tasks other than work production.

Implications for Career Education

Goal-setting, at least for such groups studied in the reports described above, appears to have positive effects; it helps to increase work production and may facilitate learning the task. The utilization of goal-setting techniques is relatively simple to master and understand. Essentially, the technique consists of some variation of the following procedure:

(1) Determine how well the worker performs a task. This can be done by measuring the number of products produced, the time required to perform a task, or the rate of production.

(2) Tell the individual the results obtained from measuring, e.g., number produced per hour.

(3) Request the worker to set a goal for the next effort, e.g., the next hour. It will probably be helpful in actual practice to encourage the worker to set a goal that is slightly better (or at least as good as) the measured performance in early stages of goal-setting, because other studies (e.g. Little and Cohen, 1951) have suggested that unusually high or unusually low goals may not be optimal. At later times, when the worker nears the upper limits of ability, perhaps goals should be at approximately the same level as prior performance, or even slightly below prior performance on tasks where fatigue may be a factor. Research on these latter suggestions is not available, but it seems reasonable to take such an approach. In relation to the potential benefits for disabled workers, it is remarkable that these techniques have not been more widely used in work settings.

By teaching students and workers who have disabilities which prevent them from competing with normal workers to effectively use goal-setting techniques, workshop and vocational teachers may be able to help such workers narrow the gap between business and industry expectations for quality and quantity of work and what the individual handicapped worker can do.

REFERENCES

Armstrong, D.E., Performance as a function of expressed and nonexpressed levels of aspiration. Unpublished master's thesis, Howard University, 1947.

Bialer, I., Conceptualization of success and failure in mentally retarded and normal children, *Journal of Personality,* 1971, 39, 407-19.

Fryer, F.W., *Evaluation of level of aspiration as a training procedures,* Inglewood Cliffs, New Jersey: Prentice-Hall, 1964.

Gardner, D.C., Goal-setting, locus of control and work performance of mentally retarded adults, *Dissertation abstracts international,* 1974, 35 (2), No. 74-17924.

Gardner, D.C., and Gardner, P.L., Goal setting and learning in the high school resource room, *Adolescence,* (In press).

Gardner, D.C., and Warren, S.A., Effects of goal setting on work performance of retarded adults and college students differing in locus of control, *Rehabilitation Psychology,* (In press).

Gardner, D.C., Warren, S.A., and Gardner, P.L., Locus of control and law knowledge: a comparison of normal, retarded and learning disabled adolescents, *Adolescence,* 1977, 12 (45), 103-109.

Kausler, D.H., Aspiration level as a determinant of performance, *Journal of Personality,* 1959, 27, 356-361.

Kliebhan, J.M., Effects of goal setting and modeling on job performance of retarded adolescents, *American Journal of Mental Deficiency,* 1967, 72, 220-226.

Lewin, K., Dembo, T., Festinger, L., Sears, P., Level of aspiration in: J. McV. Hunt (ed.) *Personality and the behavior disorders,* New York: Ronald Press, 1944, 333-378.

Little, S.W., and Cohen, L.D., Goal setting behavior of asthmatic children, and of their mothers for them, *Journal of Personality,* 1951, 19, 376-389.

Lockette, R.E., The effect of level of aspiration upon the learning of skills, Unpublished Doctoral Dissertation, University of Illinois, 1956.

Rethingshafer, D., *Motivation as related to personality,* New York: McGraw-Hill Book Company, Incorporated, 1963, 185-217.

Ricciuti, H.N., *A review of procedural variations in level of aspiration studies,* Published in San Antonio: Lackland Air Force Base, Human Resources Center, Bulletin 51-24, 1954.

Rotter, J.B., Level of aspiration as a method of studying personality Part I. A critical review of methodology, *Psychological Review,* 1942, 49, 463-474.

Rotter, J.B., *Social learning and clinical psychology,* New York: Prentice-Hall, 1954.

Warner, D.A., and DeJung, J.E., *Goal-setting behavior as an independent variable related to the performance of educable mentally retarded male adolescents on educational tasks of varying difficulty:* final report, Published in Washington, D.C.: United States Department of Health, Education and Welfare, project No. 7-1-115, 1969.

Chapter VIII
Focus on Needs: Planning Curricula

This chapter briefly outlines the career education curriculum development and infusion process. The emphasis is on the special considerations for disabled populations. It discusses steps helpful for dealing with residential programs or other closed systems (non-integrated, special classes). Some of the early sub-stages of the curriculum process will be illustrated from recent studies (Gardner & Warren, 1976).

Definition of Curriculum

In the more traditional vein, curriculum has been synonymous with the materials, workbooks, media and textbooks used by teachers in each subject. In rejecting this narrow definition, some educators have accepted an extremely broad definition, that is, that curriculum consists of all the learning experiences of every child, whether in school or out, as long as those experiences relate to the goals of the school.

We define curriculum as any experiences which are *planned by and implemented by* the school to help children meet specific learning outcomes which have been deduced from the philosophy and goals for the school. Experiences do not have to take place in the classroom or on school property.

A more narrow definition of curriculum would separate curriculum from instruction, leading to a restricted definition of "specific, organized, sequential series of learning outcomes for pupils, the *input* into the instructional system." Instruction then would be defined as the learning experiences provided the student in an educational environment (i.e., classroom) by the teacher. In the more narrow definitions of the terms, "curriculum" and "instruction," the teacher specifies the methods and most of the instructional materials while the curriculum is concerned only with the specification of student outcomes. Such definitions seem unnecessarily restricted.

Since career education curriculum infusion is concerned with not only the *objectives* (outcomes) of the educational process but also with the *instructional strategies* and the choices of *educational settings,* we have chosen the broader definition of curriculum. Our definition of curriculum includes the specifications of some, but not all, of the teaching methods and educational settings. In the context of career education curriculum infusion, for instance, the specification of instructional strategies by the curriculum would obligate the teacher to develop and utilize methods for motivating students to learn academics by emphasizing, where appropriate, the relationship of the academic subject matter to the world of work and various career choices. Moreover, the curriculum, as it relates to career education objectives, would specify alternate educational settings in the community, such as work observation stations, work/study stations, and on-the-job training programs. The curriculum infusion process would also include a cross-discipline approach (Antonellis & James, 1973) and the utilization of the career cluster concept in curriculum planning.

The Cluster Concept and the Curriculum Process

Chapter I suggested that the adoption of the USOE 15 Career Cluster System is a viable solution to the problem of how to deal with the more than 20,000 jobs identified by the Department of Labor. The fifteen occupational cluster system provides a framework around which curriculum and instructional activities can be developed. Many public schools use the USOE 15 cluster system as a means to orient elementary students to all clusters (Career Awareness Stage). At the middle school or junior high school level, students usually focus on exploring several clusters in depth (Career Exploration Stage) and by grades 11 and 12, individual students concentrate on developing entry level job skills, or prepare for a post-high school training program, in one cluster (Career Preparation Stage).

One of the problems in using the career cluster approach in special education is determination of those clusters, and levels of a particular cluster, that are appropriate for use with individuals having different disabilities. In the context of starting a career education program within a program for disabled students, there are many factors upon which the career education curriculum decisions (judgments) may be made by the curriculum development personnel, including those decisions related to cluster selection and emphasis.

Some of the more important questions are:

1. What is the job market outlook, locally and nationally, for each cluster as it relates to the specific disabled population of the individual school or program?

2. What is the interest of the students in the program of this specific school in enrolling in specific vocational training programs?

3. What abilities and handicapping conditions of this particular population might affect job entry and job performance?

4. How successful have alumni (assuming the alumni are representative of the current school population) been occupationally by cluster? Do they go to work? Do they progress on the job? Are they satisfied? What kinds of jobs do they get? In what clusters?

The answers to these, and other pertinent questions, must be obtained, organized and analyzed, *before* a residential program for disabled students can define its career education needs, develop its career education objectives and begin cross-discipline planning. Table VIII-1 illustrates the critical paths that curriculum development personnel should follow.

TABLE VIII-1
Career Education Curriculum Development
and Infusion Process

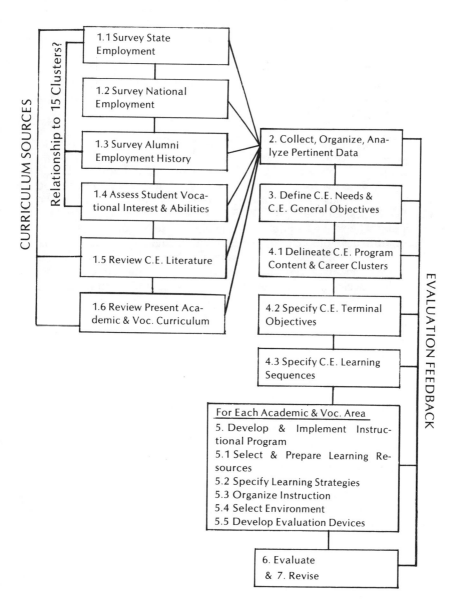

Note that items 1.1 through 1.4 are critical to the decision-making process concerning career cluster selection and organization. The balance of this chapter consists of three sections which illustrate steps 1.1 to 1.3: (1) surveying the state employment picture for a handicapped population; (2) surveying the national employment picture for handicapped persons; (3) surveying alumni employment history in a residential school for the physically handicapped. The area (1.4) concerned with assessing vocational interest and abilities of students in a residential school for the handicapped has been discussed previously.

The idea here is to illustrate how data can be gathered and analyzed in such a manner that curriculum decisions can be based *in part* on such information. These illustrations are offered as working models. Practitioners should recognize that each institution or program is unique and that each survey section of the needs assessment process will have to be individually designed for maximum results.

Almost any job listed in the *Dictionary of Occupational Titles* probably can be performed by some disabled persons, depending upon the disabling condition and the individual's training and ability. The "listings" of jobs in the following illustrations are not meant to be restrictive or exclusive. What they represent, however, is raw data which curriculum personnel can utilize in the decision making process. These data are particularly helpful when determining clusters to be considered for training program development and for levels of clusters to emphasize. It is obvious, for example, that if a residential school or a Special Education Program has mentally retarded clients exclusively, the school or program curriculum decisions about cluster levels will be limited to those clusters of occupations not requiring a university education. Similarly, it is just as obvious that some occupations will require full use of legs and arms, thus eliminating some otherwise qualified, physically handicapped persons.

ILLUSTRATION I: SURVEYING THE STATE EMPLOYMENT PICTURE*

The purposes of this survey were to (1) determine the nature (e.g., size, type of industry, etc.) of businesses in the state which tend to hire handicapped workers, (2) to compare these firms with those who do not hire handicapped workers (3) to obtain an indication of the specific types of jobs in which physically handicapped workers were currently working in the state, (4) to determine estimates of the possible barriers to employment of physically handicapped persons in the state.

---

*Illustrations are taken from a recent study by the authors: Gardner, D.C. and Warren, S.A. *Career education potential for students at the Mass. Hospital School.* Canton, Mass.: Blue Hills Regional Technical School, 1974. (Final Report).

Method

In the summer of 1974, Queries were sent to the chief executive officer of 434 firms in the state, using an offset-printed cover letter on letterhead stock, a printed survey instrument and a pre-addressed return envelope. The mailing list for the sample was developed by random selection of names of three firms from each column on each page in the following directories:**

1. Dun & Bradstreet's *Million Dollar Directory* (1974)
2. Dun & Bradstreet's *Middle Market Directory* (1974)
3. The Greater Boston Chamber of Commerce's *1971-72 Directory of Manufacturers in Greater Boston.*

Each survey instrument sent to each selected organization was assigned a code which incorporated that organization's Standard Industrial Classification (SIC) Code for later identification and analysis. The Standard Industrial Classification Codes used in this study were based on the codes prepared by the Technical Committee on Standard Industrial Classification, under the sponsorship and supervision of the Office of Statistical Standards of the Bureau of the Budget, Executive Office of the President of the U.S.A. (1967, 1972 Revisions). Each SIC number shows the function or type of operation (i.e., goods produced, for example in "2361" (manufacturer of apparel) "6" = Girls', Children's, and infants' outerwear, and "1" = product manufactured, "dresses, blouses, waists and skirts.").

The instrument was labeled "Confidential—for research purposes only." The one-page instrument requested information on four questions and data on informant:

A. Total number of employees.
B. Total number of physically handicapped employees.
C. Listing of the type(s) of job(s) being performed by physically handicapped employee(s).
D. A section in which those firms *not* employing physically handicapped workers were asked to circle the numbers of the items listed below which applied to their policy:
   1. We would employ qualified handicapped persons if they applied.
   2. There are certain architectural prohibitions (e.g., no wheel chair ramps, elevators, etc.). Please specify.
   3. Most of the jobs are too dangerous for physically handicapped workers. Please give examples.
   4. Would depend on the degree and type of physical handicap.
   5. Other (explain).
E. Position or Title of Person Completing the Form.

Results and Discussion

Of the 434 surveys mailed, 27 were returned undeliverable by the post office. Of 95 survey instruments which were returned, one reported

**All directories were the most current available.

having "no employees" so there were 94 usable returns. Usable return rate was 23.3%.

Of the organizations responding (N = 94), 22 (23.4%) reported having physically handicapped employees. However, four firms classified deaf persons as physically handicapped and one firm so classified a blind person. The number of responding firms having workers who are physically handicapped as the term is usually defined, was 17 (18.1%). This means that of the 406 organizations actually surveyed, only 4.2% reported having physically handicapped employees.

The response rate of 23% is rather low for a mailed questionnaire, even though this one was deliberately simplified so that it could be completed in a very brief time. Although caution must be used in interpretation, this rather low return rate for mailed questionnaires suggests a low interest in recruiting physically handicapped employees, despite publicity on the topic.

Interestingly, the larger firms were more likely than small ones to report hiring physically handicapped persons; however, the total proportion of their employees with handicaps was quite low. Thus, one can conclude that the job market remains limited and it will be necessary to work hard to place physically handicapped persons in the job market. Table VIII-2 indicates the support for this conclusion:

TABLE VIII-2

Responses to Questions on Organizational Policy
on Hiring Physically Handicapped (PH) Workers

N = 94

ITEM	N	PER CENT
1. Not now employing PH workers	77	81.9%
2. Would employ qualified PH workers if applied	26	27.7%
3. Might employ PH workers under certain conditions	20	21.3%
4. Cannot or would not employ PH workers	31	33.0%
TOTAL respondents who do employ and those who would or might employ PH workers	63	67.0%

In Table VIII-3, below, job titles of the physically handicapped workers reported by the employers surveyed are listed by USOE Career Cluster, D.O.T. code, S.I.C. code and type of industry:

TABLE VIII-3

JOB TITLES OF PHYSICALLY HANDICAPPED WORKERS REPORTED BY RESPONDENTS BY S.I.C. CODE, TYPE OF INDUSTRY, D.O.T. CODE AND USOE 15 CAREER CLUSTER CATEGORY

Job Title	D.O.T.[b] CODE	USOE Career Cluster[c]	S.I.C.[a]	Type of Industry
Estimator (project management)	160.288	Construction	1542	Contract Construction
Messenger	230.878	Manufacturing	2095	Manufacturer of roasted coffee
Dunning supervisor (office)	240.368	Manufacturing	2335	Mgr. of Women's, Misses, Jr. dresses
Typist-transcriber	203.588	Manufacturing	2631	Mgr. paperboard mills
Sales, service mgr. & production scheduler	187.168 221.168	Manufacturing	2631	Mgr. paperboard mills
Foreman, water dept.	851.138	Manufacturing	2631	Mgr. paperboard mills
Laborer	534.782	Manufacturing	2641	Mgr. paper coating & glazing
Laborer	534.782	Manufacturing	2641	
Quality control supervisor	012.168	Communications & Media	2751	Commercial printing (letterpress)
Binder operator	787.782	Comm. & Media	2751	
Stainer operator	970.381	Comm. & Media	2751	
Stockroom clerk (maintenance)	223.387	Comm. & Media	2751	
Draftsman	007.281	Manufacturing	2821	Mfr. plastics, synthetic resins, etc.
Inspector-assembly	789.684	Manufacturing	3199	Mfr. leather goods
Inspector-assembly	789.684	Manufacturing	3199	Mfr. leather goods
Machine assembler	706.781	Manufacturing	3443	Mfr. fabricated plate
Draftsman	007.281	Manufacturing	3443	Manufacturer
Clerk	209.388	Manufacturing	3443	Manufacturer
Machine shop laborer	600.280	Manufacturing	3613	Mfr. switchboard & switchgear
Machine operator	600.280	Manufacturing	3613	Mfr. switchboard & switchgear
Subassembler	706.381	Manufacturing	3613	Mfr. switchboard & switchgear
Secretary	201.368	Manufacturing	3613	Mfr. switchboard & switchgear
Bank teller	212.368	Marketing & Distribution	6025	Nat'l bank, member Federal Reserve System
Partner, securities & commodities	188.168	Marketing & Dist.	6281	Services allied w/exchange of securities & commodities
Editor	132.038	Business & Office	7399	Bus. services, n.e.c.
Editor	132.038	Business & Office	7399	Bus. services, n.e.c.

a = Standard Industry Classification Code
b = **Dictionary of Occupational Titles** Code
c = 15 career clusters suggested by the United States Department of Education (USOE).

From the data collected in the state survey,* curriculum planners may conclude that the following factors appear to be important for making decisions about career clusters and vocational training to be considered for curriculum programming and job placement and counseling services at this particular residential school:

1. The Manufacturing Occupations Cluster, the Business and Office Occupations Cluster and the Communications and Media Occupations Cluster appear to be important areas for curriculum planning for physically handicapped persons.
2. Large firms in this state appear more likely to hire handicapped workers than small ones. Training programs for positions in large firms may hold a higher promise of likely employment upon graduation for physically handicapped persons in this geographical area.
3. The school program must provide professionally aggressive marketing and placement services for the graduates of its programs. The job market in this state, at least as indicated by this survey's findings, is very limited for physically handicapped workers. Increasing the number of school graduates who are successfully placed in this state's labor market will require extra effort and the services of top-flight professional placement personnel.

ILLUSTRATION II: SURVEYING THE NATIONAL EMPLOYMENT PICTURE FOR PHYSICALLY HANDICAPPED PERSONS.

The purpose of this survey, as related to the total curriculum development and decision-making process for this illustrative residential school for the physically handicapped, was to (1) determine specific job patterns (organized by the USOE 15 Career Cluster System) of physically handicapped persons who are successfully employed, and (2) study the relationships of specific handicapping conditions and types of employment.

Method

In the summer of 1974, a survey instrument was mailed to 51 Executive Directors of the National Easter Seal Society *(Directory of State Societies for Crippled Children & Adults, 1973)* and to the 50 State Commissioners of Education in the United States *(The World Almanac, 1974)*. The instrument requested that each Director or Commissioner list the names of occupations at which they had found physically handi-

---

*Data and conclusions from this survey, or any individual survey reported in this text, are not intended to be used in isolation from data and conclusions from congruent surveys and/or the review of literature.

capped persons to be most successful, coded by handicapping condition, and listed under one or more of the 15 USOE Career Clusters.

The fifteen USOE Career Clusters are:

Transportation

Communications &
  Media

Environmental Control

Consumer &
  Homemaking

Hospitality & Recreation

Fine Arts & Humanities

Marketing &
  Distribution

Agri-Business & Natural
  Resources

Business & Office

Health

Personal Service

Construction

Marine Science

Manufacturing

Public Service

(see Chapter I)

The codes used for handicapping conditions in this survey were:

WS = In Wheelchair, Self or Motor Propelled

WP = In Wheelchair, pushed by Someone

AA = Arm Amputee

LA = Leg Amputee

PC = Poor Coordination

Results

Of the 51 Executive Directors (includes Puerto Rico) to whom the survey was sent, only 12 responded. One survey was undeliverable and only 7 of the 12 returns could be tabulated because 5 returns were not completed but contained comments or attached letters. Return rate for this group was 24 per cent.

Of the 50 instruments sent to the U.S.A. State Commissioners of Education, 21 were returned for a return rate of 42%. Four returns were either filled out incorrectly or contained only comments or an attached letter. While these results cannot be considered representative of the national picture, they do provide useful data.

Table VIII-4 reports responses for the combined groups as to the frequency of occupations by the fifteen clusters.

Table VIII-5 shows jobs which are managerial, professional or technical, the number of occupations and clusters, by handicapping condition code, reported by the combined respondents. A complete list of jobs, reported by the combined respondents, coded by handicapping condition, job title, D.O.T. code and career cluster is contained in Appendix B.

TABLE VIII-4
Frequency of Responses by USOE 15
Career Clusters

USOE Career Clusters (Rank Order)	Total Jobs Listed By Respondents At Least Once
Business & Office	65
Communications & Media	52
Public Service	42
Manufacturing	40
Health	31
Personal Service	30
Transportation	28
Construction	27
Marketing & Distribution	22
Hospitality & Recreation	21
Fine Arts & Humanities	20
Consumer & Homemaking	19
Agri-Business & Natural Resources	17
Environmental Control	14
Marine Science	4

TABLE VIII-5

Proportion of Jobs Managerial, Technical & Professional, Number of Clusters and Number of Successful Occupations of Handicapped Persons as Reported by State Departments of Education and State Easter Seal Societies by Handicapping Condition Code

HANDICAPPING CONDITION CODE*

	WS	WP	AA	LA	PC
Proportion of Jobs, Manager-ial, Professional or Technical	44%	45%	49%	32%	56%
Number of Jobs	132	94	85	184	64
Number of Clusters	14	15	15	15	12

*codes:
>   WS = In Wheelchair, Self or Motor Propelled
>   WP = In Wheelchair, Pushed by Someone
>   AA = Arm Amputee
>   LA = Leg Amputee
>   PC = Poor Coordination

Discussion

An analysis of data from this survey reveals that on a national level, as reported by professional leaders in the field, physically handicapped persons are employed successfully in all fifteen of the USOE Career Clusters. The clusters most frequently reported are:

Business and Office Occupations

Communications and Media Occupations

Public Service Occupations

Manufacturing Occupations

These data are consistent with the findings of the state survey previously reported. Curriculum personnel can deduce from these findings that career education curriculum development and vocational programming would be wise to initially focus on these clusters of occupations.

In terms of the proportion of physically handicapped persons reported successfully employed in this national survey, it is noteworthy that approximately 40% of jobs reported are in the professional, managerial and technical categories of occupations. These figures suggest that of those workers who manage to become successful employees, nearly half are in the occupations which require advanced training. In other words, those physically handicapped persons who can qualify and train for professional, managerial and technical occupations seem to be employed. These data may be influenced by the level of work of the respondents to the survey, who may be more familiar with, or more likely to report high levels of work. Nevertheless, they do indicate that such work is available to qualified persons who are physically handicapped.

ILLUSTRATION III: SURVEYING ALUMNI EMPLOY-MENT HISTORY

A follow-up study, as part of the program evaluation process, is a standard procedure in vocational education. There is an extensive body of literature, both in vocational education and special education on this topic.

A potentially useful, but sometimes overlooked, tool for gathering data for curriculum decision-making, is the alumni employment history data. The assumption is made, in analyzing and applying findings of the work history of recent graduates, that these graduates probably represent the current high school student population on most characteristics. If there has been a drastic shift in student population characteristics in recent years, then such a survey may be less helpful. For instance, in the case of a school program for mentally retarded students, if the current program population has shifted markedly towards more severely retarded clients than in previous years, a follow-up study undoubtedly would yield data on the employment behavior of less severely retarded alumni. Such data would not be very useful in predicting the future employment problems of the presently more severely retarded population. With these considerations in mind, the results of a survey of the recent alumni of a hospital school for the physically handicapped is reported below as an illustration of how such techniques may be useful to the curriculum specialist.

Method

An individually typed cover letter from the superintendent of the school, a follow-up survey instrument and a stamped, pre-addressed return envelope was mailed to each graduate of the graduating classes of the previous six years (1968-1973). The sample was 65% males and 35% females. Names were from an official school list of living graduates for these years and included names, last known addresses and year of graduation.

The questionnaire items were designed to emphasize education, work histories, knowledge of job hunting procedures, and current status, including social activities. The choice of the mailed survey versus personal interview approach was made largely on the basis of efficiency.

The questionnaire was designed to provide maximal information with minimal writing by the respondent because many of the graduates of the program under study were known to have difficulty in writing. Thus, the questionnaire design focused on making the task as easy as possible mechanically. The questionnaire is shown below in Figure VIII-6.

FIGURE VIII-6

CONFIDENTIAL

Name _____   NAME OF SCHOOL HERE

Address _____   Class of 19_____

_____   Telephone_____ _____ _____

DIRECTIONS: Please complete all questions that apply.

EMPLOYMENT HISTORY

1. How many months were you employed full or part-time during the period indicated below? (Example: 1974, 3 months, clerk, XYZ Company, N. Adams, Mass., part-time). If you were in school or unemployed during these periods, please indicate in last column.

YEAR	NO. OF MOS EMPLOYED	POSITION, PLACE OF EMPLOYMENT	PART OR FULL TIME	UNEMPLOYED OR IN SCHOOL
1974				
1973				
1972				
1971				
1970				

VOCATIONAL TRAINING

2. Below is a list of types of training. Circle the letter in front of all that you have had or are now taking AND on the line behind the types of training you have had, fill in the number of the place (from the list on the right) WHERE you got the training.
EXAMPLE: A person who took bookkeeping through a correspondence course would circle the "b" in front of "Business or Commercial" and fill in a "3" on the line following "Business or Commercial."

Types of Training

a. Technical_____
   (e.g. mechanical, electrical
   computer, plumbing, etc.)
b. Business or Commercial_____
   (e.g. bookkeeping, typing,
   secretarial, etc.)
c. Academic_____
   (College or University Course Work)

Where You Took the Training

1. Vocational School
2. Apprenticeship or
   On-The-Job
3. Correspondence Course
4. Junior College
5. Four Year College
6. Other (explain) _____
   _____

3. Which one of the following types of school subjects did you find most interesting and which one least interesting? Circle the answer which indicates subject you found most interesting and cross out the subject type which you found least interesting. For example: if you found math most interesting and English least interesting, then you would circle "Math" and cross out "English."
   1. Math (arithmetic, etc.)
   2. Physical Sciences (chemistry, biology, physics, etc.)
   3. Social Sciences (history, geography, social problems, etc.)
   4. English (including literature)
   5. Foreign languages
   6. Art, music, drama
   7. Business, commercial, secretarial
   8. Vocational, technical or industrial
   9. Other (explain) _____

OTHER INFORMATION

4. How do you usually go about finding a job? (Circle those which apply.)
   a. Look at want ads in the newspapers
   b. Ask friends
   c. Ask employers
   d. Through the Massachusetts Employment Service
   e. Other (explain) _____
   What kind of work would you like to have? _____
   _____

5. Do you have a driver's license (or permit)? _____ Yes _____ No
6. Do you presently own a car? _____ Yes _____ No _____ No, but have use of one
   for employment purposes

7. You are:
   _____ A roomer _____ A renter _____ A homeowner _____ Living with family

8. Which of the following activities do you take part in *with other people?* (Circle all items that apply)
   1. Sports (e.g. golf)
   2. Outdoor activities (e.g. fishing, swimming, etc.)
   3. Indoor activities (e.g. table tennis, cards, etc.)
   4. Organized social activities (e.g. social clubs, service clubs, card clubs, church-sponsored social activities).
   5. Belong to a club or organization composed of people where I work or in my profession.
   6. Belong to a union, attend union meetings.
   7. Socialize after work with fellow workers.
   8. Other social activities (describe) _____
   What is the total number of hours you spend each week on the activities you circled on the list above? _____
9. Do you type? _____ Yes _____ No
10. What help should the government provide persons who are in any way disabled or handicapped? (Circle those that apply.)
    a. Financial assistance (money to support self and family)
    b. Medical services (diagnosis, treatment, surgery, etc.)
    c. Psychiatric, psychological treatment (help for emotional problems)
    d. Vocational counseling (to inform and help in choice of career & job)
    e. Devices (such as hearing aid, artificial limb, etc.)
    f. On-the-job training (apprenticeships)
    g. Help with finding a job
    h. Help with family problems
    i. Other (explain) _____
    j. None
11. Did you receive help in filling out this survey? _____ Yes _____ No
    If yes, give name and relationship of person assisting you with this form: _____

ADDITIONAL COMMENTS

   The questionnaire, as you can see, was divided into basically ten sections which are listed below. The emphasis in this section of Chapter VIII will be on analyzing the data that can be compared with the state and national surveys previously reported. Other data not directly concerned with the alumni employment history will not be discussed in this section.

Questionnaire Parts
   1. Employment History
   2. Vocational Training
   3. Interest in school subjects as recalled by graduate
   4. Methods used in finding jobs
   5.-6. Information about driving and owning cars
   7. Family or single living arrangements
   8. Frequency of social activities
   9. Typing ability
   10. Opinions about kinds of governmental help
   11. Open comments

Cover Letter and Follow-up Mailing

Each cover letter was individually typed on school letterhead stock (autotyping service) in order to indicate personalized interest and was signed by the school superintendent. The cover letter simply stated that the opinions of former students would provide valuable input in helping the school plan for improvements in programming. All envelopes were stamped "Confidential."

A second mailing was sent to non-respondents approximately four weeks after the first mailing. This mailing consisted of a carbon copy of the first mailing cover letter, a second copy of the follow-up instrument and a stamped return envelope. On the upper left hand corner of the carbon letter was a *handwritten* note urging the graduate to respond. An effort was made to locate students whose initial mail was returned undeliverable by the post office.

Results and Discussion

Return Rate: A total of 69 graduates were mailed letters. Of these, seven were returned by the post office and new addresses could not be determined. Thus, the actual pool of potential respondents was 62. Of these, there were 33 returns, a return rate of 53%. While this rate is consistent with reports of return rates for mailed questionnaires as reported in the literature, it is not as high as rates for individuals who are deeply concerned with the topic of the survey. (For example, a survey of psychologists asking about appropriate salary increments for colleagues employed in government agencies, yielded a remarkable 100% rate and when parents are queried about services needed for their handicapped children, it is not unusual to get 75% return rate.) Thus, one might conclude that these graduates were moderately interested, but not deeply concerned with the topic of program improvement. Another possibility, of course, could be that the difficulty some of them had with writing may have lowered the return rate.

Whatever the reason for the lower than expected return rate, it is believed that sufficient data were obtained to draw tentative conclusions. These comments should be interpreted in the light of the degree of representativeness of the sample of respondents and recognition should be given to the fact that this sample probably represents those students who feel that they have information which may be helpful and who also feel concern about helping the program.

Comparison of the groups who did and did not respond suggests that the non-respondents do differ somewhat from the respondents. Data available from files on each graduate was compiled and the respondents were compared with non-respondents on degree of ambulation. Results were as follows:

	Respondents		Non-Respondents	
	N	%	N	%
Wheelchair locomotion	26	78.8	15	51.0
On crutches	3	9.1	7	24.5
Ambulator	4	12.1	7	24.5
Total	33	100.0	29	100.0
Dual Handicaps	2	6.7	3	9.1

The respondents were more likely to be in wheelchairs, rather than on crutches or ambulatory.

Sex Differences

Of the individuals who responded to the questionnaire, 25 (75.8%) were males and 8 (25.2%) were females. This is reasonably close to the male-female distribution of the total group (65% male, 35% female) of graduates for the years surveyed. Thus, a majority of the students in this illustrative study are males. Despite Women's Liberation, the current trend still is one in which males are expected to work if they are able, and to support their families, whereas females are still "allowed" in current society to remain at home with less stigma. Furthermore, certain jobs still are seen as masculine (e.g., engineering) whereas other jobs are seen as primarily feminine (e.g., stenography). The heavy majority of males in this population must be given some consideration in any career planning and educational provisions for careers.

Geography

Current addresses for almost all the students in this alumni survey were in the state in which the school is located. The small degree of geographic mobility (only two were from out of state) suggests that training of these students may be oriented towards work in the immediate area. Thus, the state employment survey appears to be a valid one for the purposes of curriculum development and planning. The fact that most of the students live near the major metropolitan area of the state is not surprising in view of the fact that it is the hub of the state population.

Postgraduate Education

The majority of the alumni who responded to the survey reported additional education or training since graduation. Twenty-five (75.8%) alumni reported having had further vocational training. Of these, 11 reported some technical training, 5 business or commercial education, and 11 some college; two reported two types of post-high school training. At first glance, this picture appears relatively positive, but further study of the data suggested that the picture may not be so bright as first glances indicate. Of those who had some college work, many reported occasional courses rather than full enrollment. Of the 33 (college age) respondents, only 5 (15%) were full-time students who have been working on degree programs and only one of the nine students of the class of 1969 (which would have ordinarily finished college in 1972 if they went straight through) reported graduating. It would appear that the college-bound curriculum used at the school may not have been the most helpful for those who graduated in recent years.

Employment History

Findings of this survey support numerous previous reports indicating that it is difficult for the handicapped to get and keep employment in our society. Only 8 (24%) of the students reported full employment or full-time school since graduation. Eight more reported some kind of school program without employment since graduation, 3 reported periods of full-time and other periods of part-time employment, 2 were in full-time sheltered workshops. There were 4 who had no post-high school along with some part-time educational activity. One had no school, but occasional employment, and 7 had never held a job. Thus, less than half the group had been in full-time employment or full-time school since graduation; the picture is a bleak one generally.

Table VIII-7 reports the number of positions by career cluster.

TABLE VIII-7
Alumni Employment by USOE Career Cluster[a]

CAREER CLUSTER	No. of Positions
Hospitality & Recreation	2
Marketing & Distribution	1
Business & Office	2
Manufacturing	7
Health	2
Transportation	1
Marine Science	1
Public Service	8[b]
TOTAL	24

[a] There are more "jobs" than alumni reporting jobs, i.e., some alumni have held more than one job since graduation.

[b] Two alumni reported themselves as clients in sheltered workshops. Classification here is arbitrary.

Note that the alumni report working in only eight of the fifteen clusters.

Job Types

Of the jobs reported by graduates, several were related to medical or rehabilitative agencies. For example, one graduate reported working full time as a systems coordinator for the state rehabilitation commission. Another worked with the Jewish Vocational Services, another in a hospital. Other jobs reported more than once included dispatcher, clerk, and assembly line work. Table VIII-8 shows the breakdown by job type:

TABLE VIII-8

Alumni Employment by Job Type [a]

Job Type	No. of Positions
Clerical	10
Technical, skilled or manual	5
Semi-skilled to Unskilled	4
Human Services	3
Unknown [b]	2
TOTAL	24

[a] There are more "jobs" than alumni reporting jobs, i.e., some alumni have held more than one job since graduation.

[b] Two respondents reported working in a specific cluster but did not report exact job title.

Table VIII-9 summarizes the alumni employment history and includes D.O.T. codes where feasible.

Summary

The process of implementing curriculum change and reform is an exceptionally complex one. It is especially complex when compounded with the need for making special provisions for persons with mental or physical handicaps. In this chapter we have offered a model of the career education curriculum development process and have illustrated from recent research three of the early stages of the needs assessment portion of that model.

One cannot detail the entire curriculum-instructional unit development process in a brief text. There are a number of excellent general works on curriculum development (e.g., Neagley and Evans, 1967), many "special education" references on instructional unit development (e.g., Meyen, 1972), several popular works on developing instructional objectives (e.g., Mager, 1962) and a growing list of references on curriculum and materials in career education (see Appendix A).

The focus of this chapter was on illustrating three very important aspects (stages) of the needs assessment portion of the model presented in Table VIII-1, items 1.1 to 1.3. The stages were (1) surveying the state employment picture for physically handicapped persons, (2) surveying the national employment picture for physically handicapped persons, and (3) a follow-up study of recent graduates from a hospital school for the physically handicapped with emphasis on the alumni employment history.

TABLE VIII-9

Summary of Alumni Employment History: Job Title, D.O.T. Code,
USOE, 15 Career Cluster Categories and Type of Employment

JOB TITLE	D.O.T. CODE [a]	CAREER CLUSTER [b]	TYPE OF EMPLOYMENT
Recreation Director	187.118	Hospitality & Recreation	Full-time (Summer only)
Camp Counselor	159.228	Hospitality & Recreation	Full-time (Summer only)
Clerk	209.388	Marketing & Distribution	Full-time (Summer only)
Clerk	209.388	Business & Office	Full-time
Clerk	209.388	Business & Office	Full-time (Summer only)
Clerk	209.388	Manufacturing	Full-time
Secretary	201.368	Manufacturing	Full-time
Switchboard Operator	235.862	Manufacturing	Full-time
Technician	N.C [c]	Manufacturing	Full-time
Technician	N.C. [c]	Manufacturing	Full-time
Electronic Assembler	729.884	Manufacturing	Full-time
Machine Operator	619.885	Manufacturing	Full-time
Dispatcher	919.168	Health	Part-time
Systems Coordinator	N.C. [c]	Health	Full-time
Unknown	N.C. [c]	Marine Science	Full-time
Secretary	201.368	Transportation	(lasted only 2 wks.)
Surgical Technician	079.378	Public Service	Full-time
Truck Dispatcher	919.168	Public Service	Full-time
Case Worker	N.C. [c]	Public Service	Full-time
Draftsman	N.C. [c]	Public Service	Full-time
Clerk	219.388	Public Service	Full-time
Dispatcher	N.C. [c]	Public Service	Full-time
Unknown (2 alumni)	N.C. [c]	Public Service	Full-time, CLIENTS in workshops

[a] **Dictionary of Occupational Titles, Washington, D.C.** (U.S. Department of Labor, 1965, Vols. I & II).

[b] Refers to the 15 occupational clusters suggested by the U.S. Dept. of Health, Education & Welfare (see Dull, 1972; Ressler, 1973).

[c] N.C. = Not Codable—not possible to code item because of insufficient information.

Below is a summary of the findings of the three needs assessment stages as they relate to making decisions about curriculum reform in the context of the career education curriculum development process model presented in this chapter.

1. Initial Cluster Emphasis

Important areas to be considered for curriculum planning and programming are the Business and Office Occupations Cluster, the Communication and Media Occupations Cluster, the Manufacturing Occupations Cluster and the Public Services Occupations Cluster. These four clusters represent the clusters in which the larger proportion of handicapped workers in the combined surveys were reported as employed.

In the context of the findings of the alumni employment history survey, the Business and Office Occupations Cluster appears to be especially important for curriculum decision-making. This survey found that over 41% of the alumni of the school report employment in clerical occupations (see Table VIII-8, page 130).

One can deduce that secondary vocational training programs in this particular school should focus on providing students with skills in the above clusters. Also, the Business Education program, currently offered, should probably be expanded and updated.

2. Emphasis on Non-College Bound Curriculum

Only 15% of the respondents to the alumni survey actually report themselves as full-time college students (last six years graduates). Of the graduates surveyed who should have completed a four year program prior to the survey had they completed the normal four year college cycle, only one student reports having graduated. When these findings are combined with the results of the assessment of current student population, one can conclude that most of the recent graduates and the students currently enrolled will probably not enroll in or complete a four-year college program.

Thus, it appears that the majority of the students in this school would benefit from a career education program which focuses on acquiring entry level or technical skills in occupations which do not require training beyond the secondary level. This conclusion in no way implies that the school should cease to offer a college preparatory program for those whose interests and abilities would indicate such a career path.

3. The Job Market

Both the state survey and the alumni follow-up survey suggest that curriculum decisions need to include in their contingency data base the fact that most of the graduates have in the past and probably will in the future, confine their job hunting and employment activities to the local job market.

4. Sex Difference

The majority of the students in this school and in the alumni body as a whole, are males. As noted earlier, despite Women's Liberation, the current trend still is one in which males are expected to work, if able, and females can remain home with less stigma. Furthermore, there are still a number of jobs seen as primarily "masculine" and others as "feminine" by many Americans. The heavy majority of "males" in this population should be given a consideration in curriculum planning for career education in such schools.

5. College-Bound Curricula

An analysis of the data gathered from the national employment picture survey suggests that the school should plan for the fact that, regardless of handicap, a sizable proportion of the handicapped persons who were reported as being successfully employed were in managerial, technical or professional jobs, regardless of cluster. Depending upon the handicapping condition, the proportion in managerial, technical or professional positions ranged from 32% to 56% of those reported to be successfully employed. Provisions for students who have the ability and interest which indicates technical training (e.g., two-year college program) or managerial or professional training (four-year or more college program) must be included in the curriculum planning process.

6. Job Placement and Counseling Programming

In another chapter, we discussed in detail the barriers to employment for handicapped persons, in general. The surveys illustrated in this chapter reinforce the conclusion that it is very difficult for physically handicapped persons to obtain jobs. For instance, the national survey (see Table VIII-2) found that over 81% of the respondents did not employ handicapped persons and nearly 33% said they would not or could not employ them! Moreover, less than 25% of the recent graduates (last six years) of this school for physically handicapped reported themselves as being employed at all!

One can infer from both the data illustrated in the surveys in this chapter, and from the general literature, that educational programs need to provide professional, aggressive marketing and placement services for graduates of the programs as well as superior career counseling services for students. The school, then, must provide for these services as part of their curriculum development process.

REFERENCES

Dictionary of Occupational Titles, Washington, D.C.: U.S. Department of Labor, 1965 (3rd Edition) (2 Vols.).

Gardner, D.C. and Warren, S.A., Career education potential for students at the Massachusetts Hospital School in Canton. Resources in Education, June, 1976 ED 117 454.

Meyen, E.L. Developing Units of Instruction: For the Mentally Retarded and Other Children with Learning Disabilities, Dubuque, IA: Wm. C. Brown, Co., 1972.

Neagley, R.L. and Evans, N.D. Handbook for Effective Curriculum Development, Englewood Cliffs, NJ: Prentice-Hall, Inc., 1967.

Chapter IX

Last Words

Then and Now

In the early chapters of this book, emphasis is placed on applying the concepts of career education to reduce the problems of providing children with disabilities with skills needed to help them to take an effective place in society and to help them develop occupational skills. Career education as it is currently understood is described in the first chapter. Many readers will realize that all of the concepts of the career education movement are not new. For example, in the early days of this century, G. Stanley Hall held that the first aim of education of both boys and girls should be to enable pupils to earn their own living; Hall's influence was great in his day for he was the "father" of developmental psychology and one of the foremost teachers of his day. But the idea of placing first the idea of teaching children skills that would permit them to earn their own living had gradually seemed somewhat less important in the educational system.

The changes may reflect other developments in American education. In the early days of this country, even rather young children were able to help in the household and farm tasks. At about the time of the American Revolution, children learned some basic reading, writing, and arithmetic skills before they were apprenticed to masters to learn a skilled trade. The popular story of *Johnny Tremain,* who was apprentice to a silversmith, is a typical example of such vocational education.

With the expansion of free public education and the passage of compulsory education laws, a greater proportion of children were in school for more years. Classroom instruction became the most popular approach. For the small numbers of children who were blind or deaf, residential schools were founded and some vocational skills were taught to those children. A relatively small proportion of the mentally retarded (perhaps as much as 10%) were also provided with residential services. In such facilities, there was often an emphasis on learning practical, everyday skills, especially those that were useful in the residential facility. Such skills were often taught by members of the staff who were hired to do the job while the teachers on the staff were providing instruction in basic academic skills.

For the large numbers of disabled children and youth in the community, the "regular" education curricula of the classrooms was often very difficult. Special classes developed for retarded students (and for a few others), itinerant teachers were employed to work with blind children in such activities as Braille reading and use of talking books. And materials specially designed for disabled pupils were developed. Curriculum designs with less emphasis on reading from textbooks and more emphasis on units of study that had a focus on special topics developed. Frequently these units were related to the world of work; however, decisions were often those of the individual teacher, as contrasted to the more organized approch toward introduction to the world of work that career education has. Many children with disabilities dropped out of school at the first opportunity; although some found jobs, often with friends or relatives, the unemployment rate among those with disabilities has always been high for those drop-outs.

Although federal funds for vocational education have been available for many years, it was not until quite recently that the federal government mandated that some of those funds (Part B set-aside) should be used in vocational training for handicapped students. In these new programs, pre-vocational and vocational skills are stressed. Thus, one can now find in junior high and high schools some retarded, learning disabled, and hearing impaired children in work-study, on-the-job training, and cooperative education. However, many of these students have little or no introduction to the world of work before entering these programs. Most of them are still relatively new ventures for vocational programs that have been serving non-handicapped students and so the programs are still in early developmental stages.

The advantages of having students spend part of their school day at a work setting are many. Students can practice in a place where immediate feedback about the work is readily possible; they can learn some of the work habits that are crucial to maintaining a job. They can earn some money. Meanwhile, at the school, they can continue to learn about government, the arts, and current events.

Advantages of the current system over the old apprenticeship include: potential for better selection of an appropriate work setting, the school as a home base gives better opportunity for monitoring the student's activities, and there is better opportunity to ensure that the student continues educational work. (Master's were enjoined to see that each apprentice attended school, but the schooling was meager and the law difficult to enforce.)

Some progress is being made, but there is still far to go. Vocational education for disabled adolescents is progress, but it is still limited and it is not comprehensive career education for them.

Accent on Working

Throughout these pages, there has been a clear indication of the belief of the authors in the dignity of work. This is not an opinion that is new or unique. Charles Darwin said that "It is well for a man to respect his vocation, whatever it is, and to think himself bound to uphold it, and to claim for it the respect it deserves." Henry Van Dyke commented: "Be glad of life because it gives you the chance to love and to work and to play and to look up at the stars." George Bernard Shaw said it this way: "Being forced to work, and being forced to do your very best, will breed in you temperance, self-control, diligence, strength of will, content, and a hundred other virtues which the idle will never know."

Another famous American recognized the dignity of all types of work. His words seem especially relevant to many of the handicapped who may be barred from the technical and professional activities. Although he wrote in a different context, Booker T. Washington's words are important to those who would help students learn the dignity of work. He said, "...we shall prosper in proportion as we learn to dignify and glorify common labor and put brains into common occupations...no race can prosper till it learns that there is as much dignity in tilling a field as in the writing of a poem."

One might add that there is greater probability of earning a living by tilling a field than in writing a poem. Sometimes one is inclined to think of work as "Paid employment," meaning work for a pre-determined amount of money. It requires little thought to remind ourselves that much work is unpaid: housewives, mothers, and Saturday afternoon gardeners are not paid in money. One man's hobby is another man's work...photography, writing, art, greenhouse activities, winemaking, football playing...and vice versa.

Perhaps we speak too much of the dignity of work and too little of the dignity of leisure. There is dignity in both. Perhaps if one thinks of work as gainful and meaningful activity without insisting that gainful means money, the picture will become clearer. Work may be any activity that is useful to the individual or to others. There are individuals whose disabilities are so handicapping that the potential for paid employment is very low. Such individuals can, however, engage in meaningful and useful work and it may be good education and good counseling to aid them to learn to do so. The basis for this statement is suggested in the quotation below from an editorial in *Mental Retardation:*

Of Pride and Peonage

Le fruit du travail est le plus des plaisirs

Among the several class action suits filed on behalf of the retarded in recent years are suits charging certain institutional administrators with the practice of peonage. ...It may be appropriate to comment on the meaning of the word "peonage" and on the dignity of work. Peonage is defined as a system of compulsory labor based on indebtedness by the worker to an employer and a legal obligation to remain in service until the debt is paid. Unlike slavery and penal servitude, peonage implies a contractual relationship. Thus, it is similar to the system of indentured servitude that brought so many of our ancestors to America....

Work, in institutions or elsewhere, is not often described as a major source of pride and thus worthwhile even in the absence of remuneration. Yet many people work for no pay. Volunteers. Consulting editors. Committee members. AAMD officers....

Perhaps it is worthwhile considering work as a source of pride for retarded individuals, too. Both common sense and psychological experiments suggest to us that the retarded have met many failures and few successes; such a history decreases efforts and provides limited reward. For some adults in institutions, the work activity is the highlight of the day because it provides a very real feeling of achievement, a realization that one is needed and useful, a proud moment. Need for achievement and pride in achievement can be found at all ages, all intellectual levels, all financial stages.... Perhaps it is not work (with or without money), but attitudes toward work that make a difference, for young and old, retarded and average people. Enforced work seen as menial can be exploitation; the same work seen as helping others is not.

Nothing can excuse exploitation of one human being by another. Neither should one ignore the fact that, as the French say, the fruit of toil is the sweetest of pleasures. (Warren, 1973, p.2)

If Given Opportunities...

It has been noted repeatedly that the unemployment rate (at paying jobs) is high for disabled persons. However, there is evidence that handicapped persons can be excellent employees. The President's Committee on Employment of the Handicapped has published a number of booklets and brochures that discuss that point and that give data on studies on handicapped employees. For example, one leaflet, "Hiring the Handicapped: Facts and Myths," cites an eight-month study by the du Pont company of 1,452 employed who had such handicapping conditions as orthopedic problems, blindness, heart disease, amputations, paralysis, epilepsy, and hearing handicaps. Key findings of that study included: No increase in compensation costs or lost-time due to injuries, no special work arrangements needed for most of these employees, safety records showed 96% rated average-or-better both on and off the job, job performance ratings indicated that 91% were rated average-or-better, on attendance 79% rated average-or-better, and the handicapped persons were able to work in harmony with supervisors and fellow employees. Data from other studies cited in the same materials indicated high productivity, relatively low accident rates, low absentee and turnover rate, and generally favorable performance as compared with non-handicapped workers. In those jobs that are not precluded by the handicapping condition, work is reported as competitive. It has been noted in other chapters that some types of activity cannot be performed because of the disability. Visual handicaps make some jobs out of reach (e.g., airline pilot or navigator), about three-fourths of mentally retarded workers are in service work or industrial jobs, locomotor problems can eliminate some jobs. For some persons, no jobs at all will be possible. But each individual should have educational opportunities that will make it possible for that person to do whatever work capabilities permit.

The philanthropist George Peadbody described education as a debt due from present to future generations. Disabled students, no less than other students, deserve a chance, an adequate education for a career.

REFERENCES

Mager, R.F. *Preparing Instructional Objectives*, Palo Alto, CA: Fearon Publishers, 1962.

President's Committee on Employment of the Handicapped. *Hiring the Handicapped: Facts and Myths*. Chicago: American Mutual Insurance Co. (n.d.)

Warren, S.A. Of Pride and Peonage. *Mental Retardation*, 1973, XI,3,2.

Appendix A

I. General Reference Section in most libraries for Initial Search

1. *Bibliographic Index.* The H. W. Wilson Co., 950 University Avenue, Bronx, NY 10452.

2. *Books in Print.* R. R. Bowker Co., 1180 Avenue of the Americas, New York, NY 10036.

3. *Child Development Abstracts.* The University of Chicago Press for the Society for Research in Child Development, 5801 Ellis Avenue, Chicago, IL 60637.

4. *Current Index to Journals in Education.* MacMillan Information, division of MacMillan Publishing Co. Inc., 866 Third Avenue, New York, NY 10022.

5. *Dissertation Abstracts International.* Xerox University Microfilms, Ann Arbor, MI 48106.

6. *Education Index.* H. W. Wilson Co., 950 University Avenue, Bronx, NY 10452.

7. *Encyclopedia of Educational Research,* 4th ed., 1969. The MacMillan Co., Colheir-MacMillan Ltd., Toronto, Ontario, Canada.

8. *Psychological Abstracts.* The American Psychological Association, Inc., 1200 Seventeenth St., N.W., Washington, D.C. 20036.

9. *Resources in Education* (formerly *Research in Education*). Superintendent of Documents, U.S. Government Printing Office, Washington, D.C. 20402. (ERIC).

10. *Review of Educational Research.* American Educational Research Association, 1126 16th Street, N.W., Washington, D.C. 20036.

II. ERIC Clearinghouses

ERIC Clearinghouses acquire, review and index journal articles announced in Current *Index to Journals in Education.* Also, each of the 16 ERIC Clearinghouses prepare bibliographic citations and abstracts of research documents which are announced in *Resources in Education* and disseminated through the ERIC Document Reproduction Service. Educators and other interested individuals may subscribe to RIE by writing to the Superintendent of Documents, U.S. Government Printing Office, Washington, D.C. 20402.

ERIC CLEARINGHOUSES*

ADELL   Adult Education and Lifelong Learning
204 Gabel Hall
Northern Illinois University
Dekalb, IL 60115
(815) 753-1251

CE CAREER EDUCATION
The Ohio State University
1960 Kenny Road
Columbus, OH 43210
(614) 486-3655

CG COUNSELING AND PERSONNEL SERVICES
University of Michigan
Ann Arbor, MI 48104
(313) 764-1817

CS READING AND COMMUNICATION SKILLS
National Council of Teachers of English
Urbana, IL 61801
(217) 328-3870

EA EDUCATIONAL MANAGEMENT
University of Oregon
Eugene, OR 97403
(503) 686-5043

EC HANDICAPPED AND GIFTED CHILDREN
The Council for Exceptional Children
Reston, VA 22091
(703) 620-3660

FL LANGUAGES AND LINGUISTICS
Center for Applied Linguistics
Arlington, VA 22209
(703) 528-4312

HE HIGHER EDUCATION
George Washington University
Washington, D.C. 20006
(203) 296-2597

IR INFORMATION RESOURCES
Stanford University
Stanford, CA 94305

JC JUNIOR COLLEGES
University of California at Los Angeles
Los Angeles, CA 90024
(213) 825-4321

*Addresses and telephone numbers as of April 1977.

PS EARLY CHILDHOOD EDUCATION
University of Illinois
Urbana, IL 61801
(217) 333-4666

RC RURAL EDUCATION AND SMALL SCHOOLS
New Mexico State University
Las Cruces, NM 88001
(505) 646-0111

SE SCIENCE MATHEMATICS AND ENVIRONMENTAL EDUCATION
The Ohio State University
Columbus, OH 43221
(614) 422-6446

SO SOCIAL STUDIES/SOCIAL SCIENCE EDUCATION
Social Science Education Consortium, Inc.
Boulder, CO 90302
(303) 492-0111

SP TEACHER EDUCATION
American Association of Colleges for Teacher Education
Washington, D.C. 20005
(202) 293-7280

TM TESTS, MEASUREMENT, AND EVALUATION
Educational Testing Service
Princeton, NJ 08540
(609) 921-9000

UD DISADVANTAGED
Teachers College
Columbia University
New York, NY 10027
(212) 678-3000

III. USOE Career Education Models

A. *School-Based*
The Center for Vocational and Technical Education
The Ohio State University
1960 Kenny Road
Columbus, OH 43210
(614) 486-3655

B. *Experience-Based*
Appalachia Educational Laboratory
Box 1348
Charleston, WV
(304) 344-8371

Far West Laboratory for Educational Research and Development
1855 Folsom Street
San Francisco, CA
(415) 565-3000

*Addresses and telephone numbers as of April 1977.

Northwest Regional Educational Laboratory
710 S.W. Second Avenue
Portland, OR 97204
(503) 248-6800

Research for Better Schools, Inc.
1700 Market Street
Suite 1700
Philadelphia, PA 19103
(215) 561-4100

C. *Home-Based Community-Based*
Education Development Center, Inc.
55 Chapel Street
Newton, MA 02158
(617) 969-7100

Southwestern Cooperative Educational Laboratory
1404 San Matel Boulevard, S.E.
Albuquerque, NM 87108
(505) 268-3348

D. *Rural Residential-Based*
Mountain Plains Educational and Economic Development Program, Inc.
Glasgow Air Force Base
Glasgow, MT
(406) 524-3630

*Addresses and telephone numbers as of April 1977.

IV. Vocational-Technical Education

NATIONAL NETWORK FOR CURRICULUM COORDINATION

	CENTERS	SERVICE AREAS
CALIFORNIA	Dr. James Becket, Director Western Curriculum Coordination Center Vocational Education Department of Education 721 Capitol Mall Sacramento, California 95814 (916) 322-2330	American Samoa, Arizona, California, Guam, Hawaii Nevada, Trust Territory of Pacific Islands
ILLINOIS	Rebecca S. Douglass, Director East Central Curriculum Coordination Center, Processional and Curriculum Development Unit, Division of Voca- tional-Technical Education 1035 Outer Park Drive Springfield, Illinois 62706 (217) 782-7084	Delaware, District of Columbia, Indiana, Illi- nois, Maryland, Michigan, Minnesota, Ohio, Penn- sylvania, Virginia, West Virginia

MISSISSIPPI   Dr. James E. Wall, Director
Southeast Curriculum Coordination
Center, Mississippi State University
Research and Curriculum Unit
Drawer JW
Mississippi State, MS 39762
(601) 325-2510

Alabama, Florida, Georgia
Kentucky, Mississippi,
North Carolina, South
Carolina, Tennessee

NEW JERSEY   Dr. Joseph F. Kelly, Director
Northeast Curriculum Coordination
Center, Bureau of Occupational Research
Division of Vocational Education
225 West State Street
Trenton, New Jersey 98625
(609) 292-6562

Connecticut, Maine, Mas-
sachusetts, New Hamp-
shire, New Jersey, New
York, Puerto Rico, Ver-
mont, Virgin Islands

OKLAHOMA   Robert Patton, Director
Midwest Curriculum Coordination
Center, State Department of Vocational
and Technical Education
1515 West 6th Avenue
Stillwater, Oklahoma 74074
(405) 377-2000—Ext. 260

Arkansas, Iowa, Kansas,
Louisiana, Missouri,
Nebraska, New Mexico,
Oklahoma, Texas

WASHINGTON   William Daniels, Director
Northwestern Curriculum Coordination
Center, Washington State Coordinating
Council for Occupational Education
222 Airdustrial Park
Box 17
Olympia, Washington 98504
(206) 753-5662

Alaska, Colorado, Idaho,
Montana, North Dakota,
Oregon, South Dakota,
Utah, Washington,
Wyoming

V. Other Federal Government Resources and Agencies

A. United States Office of Education
Office of Career Education
400 Maryland Avenue, S.W.
Washington, D.C. 20202
(202) 245-8710

B. To receive new publications and information bulletins (free)
send name and address to:
Superintendent of Documents
U.S. Government Printing Office
Box 1821
Washington, D.C. 20013

C. National Institute of Education (NIE)
1200 19th Street, N.W.
Washington, D.C. 20208

D. National Advisory Council for Career Education
   Office of Education, DHEW
   Washington, D.C. 20202

E. Bureau of Education for the Handicapped
   400 Mailand Avenue, SW
   Washington, DC 20202

F. President's Committee on Employment of the Handicapped
   1111 20th Street, NW
   Washington, DC 20210

VI. Selected Professional Associations

National Association for Career Education
Glassboro State College
Glassboro, NJ 08028

American Personnel & Guidance Association
1607 New Hampshire Avenue, NW
Washington, DC 20009

American Vocational Association
1201 16th Street, N.W.
Washington, D.C. 20005

Council for Exceptional Children
1920 Association Drive
Reston, VA 22091

American Association on Mental Deficiency
5101 Wisconsin Avenue, NW
Washington, DC 20016

National Business Education Association
Dulles International Airport
P.O. Box 17402
Washington, D.C. 20041

VII. Bibliographies

A. Selected bibliographies, Boston University, Department of Business and Career Education.

   1. Working Bibliography: Typewriting for the Learning Handicapped Student. Marilyn Zwicker, Judith Mazza, and Margaret Kurtz (VITA).

   2. Working Bibliography: Teaching Vocabulary to Learning Handicapped Students. Prepared by Libby Cohen, directed by Margaret Kurtz (VITA).

   3. Working Bibliography: Tests Related to the Measurement of Career Maturity. Wayne Dimetres, Margaret Kurtz and Harold Resnick (VITA).

   4. Working Bibliography: Vocational Instruction, Training, and Assessment for Students with Special Needs. Thomas L. Wilton and Paula Barron (VITA).

5. Working Bibliography: Departmental reserve list: Career Education Texts (annotated, in press).

6. Working Bibliography: Sex Stereotyping in the Middle Schools, (annotated). Thomas L. Wilton.

B. Selected ERIC Bibliographies

An annotated bibliography of selected career education materials and references for physically handicapped students. In: Gardner, D. C. and Warren, S. A. *Career education potential for students at the Massachusetts Hospital School,* pp. 145-162, ERIC ED117454.

Career Development Resources: A bibliography of audiovisual and printed materials K-12, ED117292.

Career Education: An annotated bibliography for teachers and curriculum developers. (January, 1973) ERIC ED073297.

Career Education: A bibliography of resources. ED103609.

Career Education, an ERIC bibliography. New York: MacMillan Information, 1973.

Career Education Materials for Educable Retarded Students Working Paper No. 6. ED116443.

A Career Education Primer for Educators. Information Series #4 ED113486.

Career Education Resource Bibliography. ED117548.

Dunn, J. A. & others. *Career Education: An annotated bibliography for teachers and curriculum developers.* Palo Alto, California, American Institute for Research, 1973.

High, D. C., Jr. & Hall, L. *Bibliography on career education: working paper.* Washington, D.C.: Bureau of Adult, Vocational, and Technical Education, 1972 (ED-070822).

Mathusin, M. B. *A bibliography of bibliographies on career and vocational education:* Part II of the ERIC Clearinghouse on teacher education project on career education. Washington, D.C.: ERIC Clearinghouse on Teacher Education, 1972. ED-067387.

1900 Doctoral Dissertations on Career Education ED121933.

A Selected bibliography of ERIC Career Education, Career Guidance, and Career Development Resources. ED108099 ERIC Clearinghouse on Counseling & Personnel Services, Ann Arbor, Michigan.

A Selected bibliography for Vocational Training and placement of the severely handicapped. Project (VOTAP) ED116436.

A Total Community Approach to Career Education. Resources for Career Development: an annotated bibliography (revised) ED117361.

VIII. List of Journals and Periodicals

Adolescence
William Kroll, Editor-in-Chief
Libra Publisher, Inc.
P.O. Box 165
391 Willets Road
Roslyn Heights, NY 11577

Adult Education
Gordon G. Darkenwald, Editor
Adult Education Association of U.S.A.
810 18th Street, N.W.
Washington, DC 20006

American Annals of the Deaf
McCay Vernon, Editor
Department of Psychology
Western Maryland College
Westminster, MD 21157

American Education
William A. Horn, Editor
Superintendent of Documents
U.S. Government Printing Office
Washington, DC 20402

American Educational Research Journal
MaryEllen McSweeney, Editor
College of Education
Arizona State University
Tempe, AZ 85281

American Journal of Mental Deficiency
(a publication of AAMD)
H. Carl Haywood, Editor
P.O. Box 503
Peabody College
Nashville, TN 37203

American School Board Journal
David L. Martin, Managing Editor
800 State National Bank Plaza
Evanston, IL 60201

American Sociological Review
Morris Zelditch, Jr.
Department of Sociology
Stanford University
Stanford, CA 94305

American Vocational Journal
Lowell A. Burkett, Editor
1510 H Street NW
Washington, DC 20005

Audiovisual Instruction
Howard Hitchins, Editor
1201 16th Street NW
Washington, DC 20036

The Balance Sheet
Wayne K. Mayes, Editor
South-Western Publishing Company
5101 Madison Road
Cincinnati, OH 45227

Behavior Research and Therapy
H. J. Eysenck, Editor-in-Chief
Institute of Psychiatry
Department of Psychology
De Crespigny Park Road
Denmark Hill, London SE5 8AZ

British Journal of Education Psychology
N. J. Entwistle, Editor
Scottish Academic Press
33 Montgomery Street
Edinburgh, Scotland EH7 5JX

Business Education Forum
O. J. Burnside, Jr., Editor
c/o National Business Education
    Association
1906 Association Drive
Reston, VA 22091

Business Education World
Susan Schrumpf, Editor
1221 Avenue of the Americas
New York, NY 10020

Career Development for
    Exceptional Individuals
Charles Kokaska, Editor
1920 Association Drive
Reston, VA 22091

Career Education News
Bernadette Doran, Editor
155 Waukegan Road
Glenview, IL 60025

Career Education Quarterly
David C. Gardner, Editor
(A publication of the NACE)
765 Commonwealth Avenue
Boston, MA 02215

Career Education Workshop
Muriel S. Karlin, Editor
Parker Publishing Co., Inc.
West Nyack, NY 10994

Career World
Donna Cousins, Editor
Curriculum Innovators, Inc.
501 Lake Forest Avenue
Highwood, IL 60040

Child Development
Wendell E. Jeffrey, Editor
(Society for Research in Child Dev.)
University of Chicago Press
5801 Ellis Avenue
Chicago, IL 60637

Citizen Action in Education
Barbara Prentice, Editor
Institute for Responsive Education
704 Commonwealth Avenue
Boston University
Boston, MA 02215

The Clearing House
Janet M. Norton, Managing Editor
Heldref Publications
4000 Albermarle Street NW
Washington, DC 20016

Contemporary Psychology
Janet T. Spence, Editor
Department of Psychology
University of Texas
Austin, TX 78712

Contemporary Sociology
Bennett M. Berger, Editor
American Sociological Association
1722 N Street N.W.
Washington, DC 20036

The Counseling Psychologist
John M. Whitely, Editor
American Psychological Association
Washington University
Box 1053
St. Louis, MO 63130

Counselor Education and Supervision
Chris Kenas, Editor
American Personnel and Guidance Assn.
1607 New Hampshire Avenue N.W.
Washington, DC 20009

Education Digest
Lawrence W. Prakken, Editor
Prakken Publications, Inc.
P.O. Box 623
416 Longshore Drive
Ann Arbor, MI 48107

Education for the Disadvantaged Child
Juanita Chambers, Editor
University of Alberta
Department of Educational Psychology
Edmonton Alta
T6G 2G5
Edmonton Alta
Canada

Education and Training of the Mentally
    Retarded
(A publication of the Council for
    Exceptional Children)
Floyd McDowell, Editor
1920 Association Drive
Reston, VA 22091

Educational and Psychological
    Measurement
W. Scott Gehman
Box 6907 College Station
Durham, NC 27708

Exceptional Child Education Abstracts
June B. Jordon, Editor
Council for Exceptional Children
1920 Association Drive
Reston, VA 22091

Exceptional Children
M. Angele Thomas, Editor
(A publication of the Council for
    Exceptional Children)
1920 Association Drive
Reston, VA 22091

Exceptional Parent
Stanley Klein, Lewis Klebenoff, Editors
Psych-Education Corporation
264 Beacon Street 4th floor
Boston, MA 02116

Gifted Child Quarterly
John Curtis Gowan, Editor
1426 Southwind
Westlake Village, CA 91361

Gifted Child Quarterly
National Association for Gifted
  Children
217 Gregory Drive
Hot Springs, AZ 71091

Human Development
K. P. Riegel, Editor
S. Karger AG
25 Arnold Bocklin Str.
4000 Basel 11
Switzerland

Illinois Career Education Journal
Jane Adair, Editor
Division of Vocational and Technical
  Education
1035 Outer Park Drive
Springfield, IL 62706

Industrial Education
John L. Feirer, Editor
MacMillan Professional Magazines
22 West Putnam Avenue
Greenwich, CT 06830

Industrial Education Magazine
Howard Smith, Editor
MacMillan Professional Magazine
One Faucett Park
Greenwich, CT 06830

Journal of Abnormal Psychology
Leonard D. Eron, Editor
Department of Psychology
Box 4348
University of Illinois
Chicago Circle
Chicago, IL 60680

Journal of Allied Health
J. Warren Perry, Editor
School of Health Related Professions
State University of N.Y. at Buffalo
205 Foster Hall
Buffalo, NY 14214

Journal of Applied Behavior Analysis
W. Stewart Agras, M.D., Editor
Department of Psychiatry and
  Behavioral Sciences
Stanford University
School of Medicine
Stanford, CA 94305

Journal of Applied Psychology
Edwin Fleishman, Editor
American Institutes for Research
3301 New Mexico Avenue, N.W.
Washington, DC 20016

Journal of Business Education
Robert C. Trethaway, Editor
34 North Crystal Street
East Stroudsbury, PA 18301

Journal of Career Education
H. C. Kazanas, Editor
College of Education
University of Missouri
Columbia, MO 65201

The Journal of College Student
  Personnel
Albert B. Hood, Editor
American College Personnel Assn.
1605 New Hampshire Avenue, N.W.
Washington, DC 20009

Journal of Consulting and Clinical
  Psychology
Brendan A. Maher, Editor
1120 William James Hall
Harvard University
33 Kirkland Street
Cambridge, MA 02138

Journal of Continuing Education in
  Nursing
Mrs. Kay Coraluzzo, Editor
Charles B. Slack, Inc.
6900 Grove Road
Thorofare, NJ 08086

Journal of Educational Psychology
Joanna Williams, Editor
P.O. Box 238
Teachers College
Columbia University
New York, NY 10027

Journal of Employment Counseling
David Meyer, Editor
American Personnel and Guidance
  Association, Inc.
1607 New Hampshire Avenue, N.W.
Washington, DC 20009

Journal of Industrial Teacher
    Education
Ronald W. Stadt, Editor
National Association of Industrial
    Teacher Educators
School of Technology
Purdue University
Lafayette, IN 47907

Journal of Home Economics
Mary Kay Overholt, Editor
American Home Economics Association
2010 Massachusetts Avenue, N.W.
Washington, DC 20036

Journal of Mental Deficiency
    Research
B. W. Richards, Editor
St. Lawrence's Hospital
Caterham, Surrey, England CR3 5YA

Journal of Personality
Philip R. Costanzo, Editor
P.O. Box GM
Duke Station
Durham, NC 27706

Journal of Personality Assessment
Walter J. Klopfer, Editor
7840 S.W. 51st Avenue
Portland, OR 97219

Journal of Rehabilitation
Betty Winkler Roberts, Editor
National Rehabilitation Association
1522 K Street, N.W.
Washington, DC 20005

Journal of Research in Crime and
    Delinquency
D. M. Gottfredson, Editor
National Council on Crime and
    Delinquency
Research Center
Brinley Terrace
609 2nd Street
Davis, CA 95616

Journal of Research & Development
    in Education
Joseph A. Williams, Editor
College of Education
G-3 Aderhold Building
University of Georgia
Athens, GA 30602

Journal of School Psychology
Beeman N. Phillips, Editor
College of Education
Department of Educational Psychology
The University of Texas
Austin, TX 78712

Journal of Special Education
Lester Mann, Editor
3515 Woodhaven Road
Philadelphia, PA 19154

Journal for Special Educators of the
    Mentally Retarded
Joseph Prentky & Louis Marpet, Editors
American Association of Special
    Educators
107-20 125th Street
Richmond Hill, NY 11419

Journal of Speech and Hearing Research
Thomas J. Hixon, Editor
Dept. of Speech & Hearing Sciences
University of Arizona
Tucson, AZ 85721

Journal of Vocational Behavior
Lenore W. Harmon, Editor
Academic Press, Inc.
111 Fifth Avenue
New York, NY 10003

Journal of Vocational Education
    Research
Hollie B. Thomas
202 South Woodward St.
Florida State University
Tallahassee, FL 32306

Man/Society/Technology Journal
Colleen Stamm, Editor
American Industrial Arts
    Association, Inc.
NEA Headquarters Bldg.
1201 16th Street, N.W.
Washington, DC 20036

Measurement and Evaluation in Guidance
William A. Mehrens, Editor
Michigan State University
College of Education
East Lansing, MI 48824

Media and Methods
Frank McLaughlin, Editor
North American Building
401 N. Broad Street
Philadelphia, PA 19108

Mental Hygiene
Richard Allen, Editor
1800 N. Kent Street
Arlington, VA 22209

Mental Retardation
James Brody
Pennhurst Center
Spring City, PA 19475

National Elementary Principal
Paul L. Houts, Editor
1801 North Moore Street
Arlington, VA 22209

NEBEA Bulletin
Daniel Durate, Editor
427 Orange Center Road
Orange, CT 06477

Personnel and Guidance Journal
Derald Wing Sue, Editor
(APGA)
1607 New Hampshire Avenue, N.W.
Washington, DC 20009

Phi Delta Kappan
Stanley M. Elam, Editor
8th Street Union Avenue
Bloomington, IN 47401

Psychological Bulletin
R. J. Herrnstein, Editor
Harvard University
33 Kirkland Street
Cambridge, MA 02138

The Psychological Record
Irwin S. Wolf, Editor
Kenyon College
Gambier, OH 43022

Psychological Review
George Mandler, Editor
Department of Psychology
University of California at
San Diego
La Jolla, CA 92307

Rehabilitation Counseling Bulletin
Marceline E. Jaques, Editor
(A publication of APGA)
Rehabilitation Counseling Program
Christopher Baldy Hall 416
SUNY at Buffalo
Amherst, NY 14260

Rehabilitation Literature
Helen B. Crane, Editor
National Easter Seal Society for
    Crippled Children and Adults
2023 W. Ogden Avenue
Chicago, IL 60612

Occupational Outlook Quarterly
Melvin C. Fountain, Editor
U. S. Government Printing Office
Superintendent of Documents
Washington, DC 20402

The School Counselor
Marguerite R. Carroll, Editor
Fairfield University
Fairfield, CT 06430

School Shop
Lawrence W. Prakken, Editor
Prakken Publications, Inc.
416 Longshore Drive
Ann Arbor, MI 48107

Sight Saving Review
Joseph J. Kerstein, Editor
79 Madison Avenue
New York, NY 10016

Special Education News
Trudy K. Slaughter, Editor
65 East Palantine Road
Suite 101
Wheeling, IL 60090

Teaching Exceptional Children
June B. Jordon, Editor
Council for Exceptional Children
1920 Association Drive
Reston, VA 22091

Technical Education News (free)
Susan Schrumpf, Editor
McGraw-Hill Book Co.
Gregg Community College Division
1221 Avenue of the Americas
New York, NY 10020

Technical Education Reporter
Robert B. Angus, Editor
Technical Education Research Centers
44 Brattle Street
Cambridge, MA 02138

Training
Harold Littledale, Editor
Gellert Publication Corporation
1 Park Avenue
New York, NY 10016

Training and Development Journal
Michael H. Cork, Editor
American Society for Training and
 Development
P.O. Box 5307
Madison, WI 53705

Vocational Guidance Quarterly
Daniel Sinick, Editor
1605 New Hampshire Avenue, NW
Washington, DC 20009

Worklife
Walter Wood, Editor
U.S. Government Printing Office
U.S. Department of Labor
Employment & Training Administration
Washington, DC 20213

IX. Further Readings

Arrowsmith, Sue, & Cobb, Pat. *Orientation to career education: an individualized approach.* Columbus, Ohio: Center for Vocational Education, The Ohio State University, 1975.

Bailey, Larry J., Wood, Thomas B., & Fischmar, Sharon. *Facilitating career development: annotated bibliography.* Carbondale, Illinois: Dept. of Occupational Education, College of Education, Southern Illinois University, 1974.

Bailey, Larry J., & Stadt, Ronald. *Career education.* Bloomington, Illinois: McKnight Publishing Co., 1973.

Borow, Henry. *Career guidance for a new age.* Boston, Massachusetts: Houghton, Mifflin Company, 1973.

Burkett, Lowell A. *Career education: leadership roles.* Columbus, Ohio: ERIC Clearinghouse on Vocational and Technical Education, The Ohio State University, 1973.

Burt, Samuel M. *Career education; involving the community and its resources.* Columbus, Ohio: ERIC Clearinghouse on Vocational and Technical Education, The Ohio University, 1973.

Career education: a resource guide to children's books. Tallahassee, Florida: The Career Education Curriculum Laboratory, The Career Education Center, Florida State University, 1974

Cutlip, Scott M. *Career education: communicating the concept.* Columbus, Ohio: ERIC Clearinghouse on Vocational and Technical Education, The Ohio State University, 1973.

Drier, Harry N., Martinez, Nancy, & Kimmel, Karen (eds.). *An orientation to career education: group approach introduction.* Columbus, Ohio: Center for Vocational Education, The Ohio State University, 1975.

Drier, Harry, Martinez, Nancy, & Kimmel, Karen (eds.) *Orientation to career education: a group approach: module I.—why career education?* Columbus, Ohio: Center for Vocational Education, The Ohio State University, 1975.

Drier, Harry, Martinez, Nancy, & Kimmel, Karen (eds.) *Orientation to career education: a group approach: module II—career education, theory, goals, and planning considerations.* Columbus, Ohio: Center for Vocational Education, The Ohio University, 1975.

Drier, Harry, Martinez, Nancy, & Kimmel, Karen (eds.). *Orientation to career education: a group approach: module III—focusing on supportive interests and local needs.* Columbus, Ohio: Center for Vocational Education, The Ohio State University, 1975.

Drier, Harry, Martinez, Nancy, & Kimmel, Karen (eds.). *Orientation to career education: a group approach: module IV—career education models and implementation strategies.* Columbus, Ohio: Center for Vocational Education, The Ohio University, 1975.

Drier, Harry, Martinez, Nancy, & Kimmel, Karen (eds.). *Orientation to career education: a group approach: module V—role identification in career education.* Columbus, Ohio: Center for Vocational Education, The Ohio State University, 1975.

Drier, Harry, Martinez, Nancy, & Kimmel, Karen (eds.) *Orientation to career education: a group approach: module VI—resources in career education.* Columbus, Ohio: Center for Vocational Education, The Ohio State University, 1975.

Drier, Harry N. *K-12 guide for integrating career development information.* Worthington, Ohio: Charles A. Jones Publishing Co., 1972.

Edsall, Richard H. *A guide for local program evaluation.* Columbus, Ohio: ERIC Clearinghouse on Vocational and Technical Education, The Ohio State University, 1973.

Evans, Rupert N., et al. *Career education in the middle/jr. high school.* Salt Lake City, Utah: Olympus Publishing Co., 1973.

Frantz, Nevin R. *Career clusters concepts.* Columbus, Ohio: ERIC Clearinghouse on Vocational and Technical Education, Ohio State University, 1973.

Gardner, David C., & Warren, Sue A. *Career education potential for students at the Massachusetts Hospital School in Canton.* Wakefield, Massachusetts: Gardner & Warren Research, Inc., ERIC ED117454.

Gysbert, Norman C., et al. *Career guidance.* Worthington, Ohio: Charles A. Jones Publishing Co., 1973.

Gysbert, Norman C., et al. *Developing careers in the elementary school.* Columbus, Ohio: Charles E. Merrill Publishing Co., 1973.

Haines, Peter G. *Career education: in service teacher education.* Columbus, Ohio: ERIC Clearinghouse on Vocational and Technical Education, The Ohio State University, 1973.

Hansen, L. Sunny. *Career education: teacher's responsibilities.* Columbus, Ohio: ERIC Clearinghouse on Vocational and Technical Education, The Ohio State University, 1973.

Herr, Edwin L. *Vocational guidance and human development.* Boston, Massachusetts: Houghton, Mifflin Co., 1974.

Hill, George E. *Career education; guidance in the elementary school.* Columbus, Ohio: ERIC Clearinghouse on Vocational and Technical Education, The Ohio State University, 1973.

Hills, Kenneth D. *Review analysis of sources of occupational information.* Columbus, Ohio: ERIC Clearinghouse on Vocational and Technical Education, The Ohio State University, 1973.

Hoyt, Kenneth B., et al. *Career education and the elementary school.* Salt Lake City, Utah: Olympus Publishing Co., 1973.

Hoyt, Kenneth J., & Hebeler, Jean R. *Career education for gifted and talented.* Salt Lake City, Utah: Olympus Publishing Co.

Hoyt, Kenneth B., et al. *Career education: what it is and how to do it.* 2d ed. Salt Lake City, Utah: Olympus Publishing Co., 1974.

Huber, Jake. *Career education: information resources.* Columbus, Ohio: ERIC Clearinghouse on Vocational and Technical Education, The Ohio State University, 1973.

Jesser, David L. *Career education: a priority of the chief state school officers.* Salt Lake City, Utah: Olympus Publishing Co., 1976.

Koble, D. E., Jr., & Coker, R. U. (eds.). *The role of vocational education in career education.* 5th Annual National Leadership Dev. Sem. for State Director of Vocational Education. Columbus, Ohio: The Center for Vocational and Technical Education, The Ohio State University, March,1973.

Kolstoe, Oliver, & Frey, Roger M. *High school work study program.* Carbondale, Illinois: Southern Illinois University Press, 1965.

Lederer, Muriel. *The guide to career education.* New York, N.Y.: Quadrangle Press, 1974.

Leonard, George E. *Career education: disadvantaged students.* Columbus, Ohio: ERIC Clearinghouse on Vocational and Technical Education, The Ohio State University, 1973.

McClure, Larry, & Buan, Carolyn (eds.). *Essays on career education.* Portland, Oregon: Northwest Regional Educational Laboratory, 1973. (For sale by Supt. of Docs., U.S. Government Printing Office, Washington, D.C. 24021.)

Mager, Robert F., & Beach, Kenneth M., Jr. *Developing vocational instruction.* Belmont, California: Lear Siegler, Inc./Fearon Publishers, 1967.

Maxwell, David. *Career education; curriculum materials for disadvantaged.* Columbus, Ohio: ERIC Clearinghouse on Vocational and Technical Education, The Ohio State University, 1973.

Morganstern, Murry, & Michael-Smith, Harold. *Psychology on the vocational rehabilitation of the mentally retarded.* Springfield, Illinois: Charles C. Thomas, Publisher, 1973.

Norton, Robert E. *Staff development: guidelines and procedures for comprehensive education.* Columbus, Ohio: Center for Vocational Education, The Ohio State University, 1975.

Osipow, Samuel H. *Theories of career development,* 2d ed. Englewood Cliffs, New Jersey: Prentice-Hall, Inc., 1973.

Peters, Herman J., & Hanson, James C. *Vocational guidance and career development,* 2d ed. New York: The MacMillan Company, 1971.

Questions: food for thought on collecting and using follow-up data. Tallahassee, Florida: The Career Education Curriculum Laboratory, Career Education Center, Florida State University (undated).

Ressler, Ralph. *Career education; the new frontier.* Worthington, Ohio: Charles A. Jones Publishing Co., 1973.

Robertson, Marvin, Drier, Harry, Morris, Judith, & Thompson, Joseph. *Staff awareness: racial, socio-economic sex stereotypes limit career potential.* Columbus, Ohio: Center for Vocational Education, The Ohio State University, 1975.

Stevenson, John B. *An introduction to career guidance.* Worthington, Ohio: Charles A. Jones Publishing Co., 1973.

Smith, George N. *Career education: local administration of programs.* Columbus, Ohio: ERIC Clearinghouse on Vocational and Technical Education, Ohio State University, 1973.

Smoker, David. *Career education: current trends in school policies and programs.* Arlington, Virginia: National School Public Relations Association, 1974.

Staff development program for the implementation of career education teacher's guides. Columbus, Ohio: Center for Vocational Education, The Ohio State University, 1974.

Tolbert, E. L. *Counselling for career development.* Boston, Massachusetts: Houghton, Mifflin Co., 1974.

Venn, Grant. *Man, education and work: post-secondary vocational and technical education.* Washington, D.C.: American Council on Education, 1964, 1969.

The vocational education act of 1963. Washington, D.C.: U. S. Department Health, Education and Welfare, Office of Education OE-834, March/April 1964-1965.

Walthall, Joe E., & Love, Harold D. *Habituation of the mentally retarded individual.* Springfield, Illinois: Charles C. Thomas, Publisher, 1974.

Wentling, Tim L., & Lawson, Tom E. *Evaluating occupational education and training programs.* Boston, Massachusetts: Allyn and Bacon, Inc., 1975.

Wernick, Walter. *Teaching for career development in the elementary schools.* Worthington, Ohio: Charles A. Jones Publishing Co., 1973.

Wigglesworth, D. C. (ed.). *Career education: a reader.* San Francisco, California: Canfield Press, 1975.

Zaetz, Jay. *Organization of sheltered workshop programs for mentally retarded.* Springfield, Illinois: Charles C. Thomas, Publisher, 1971.

Additional further readings:

Brolin, Donn. *Vocational preparation of retarded citizens,* New York: Merrill, 1976.

Foss, G., Bostwick, D. & Harris, J. *Problems of mentally retarded young adults and obstacles to their rehabilitation: a study of consumers and service providers.* Eugene, Oregon: Rehabilitation Research and Training Center, University of Oregon, 1978.

Irvin, Larry K., Halpern, Andrew S. & Reynolds, William M. *Social and prevocational information battery—form T.* Eugene, Oregon: Rehabilitation Research and Training Center, University of Oregon, 1978.

Kanfer, Frederick H. & Goldstein, Arnold P. *Helping People Change.* Elmsford, N.Y.: Pergamon Press, 1975.

Mittler, Peter (ed.) *Research to practice in mental retardation, Vol. II, Education and training.* Baltimore: University Park Pres, 1977.

Scott, Marvin (ed.) *The Essential Profession.* Stamford, Conn.: Greylock Publishers, 1976.

Appendix B

SUCCESSFUL OCCUPATIONS OF HANDICAPPED PERSONS AS REPORTED BY
STATE DEPARTMENTS OF EDUCATION & STATE EASTER SEAL SOCIETIES BY
D.O.T. CODE, USOE CLUSTER & HANDICAPPING CONDITION

Part A: In Wheelchair, Self or Motor Propelled

Job Title	D.O.T. Code	Cluster
Architect	001.081	Construction
Electronics technician*	003.181	Manufacturing
Radio engineer	003.187	Manufacturing
Highway designer	005.081	Transportation
Statistician	020.188	Agri-Business, etc.
Research technician	029.181	Environmental Control
Marine scientist	041.081	Marine Science
School psychologist*	045.108	Public Service
Dietician	077.168	Consumer, Homemaking
Medical technician	078.381	Health
Speech therapist*	079.108	Public Service
Recreational therapist*	079.128	Transportation
Department head, college	090.168	Fine Arts, Humanities
Teacher	091.299	Fine Arts, Humanities
Teacher	092.228	Fine Arts, Humanities
Home economist	096.128	Environmental Control
Home economics director	096.168	Environmental Control
Budget consultant	096.268	Construction
Script writer	131.088	Communications, Media
Script writer*	131.088	Communications, Media
Journalist*	132.268	Communications, Media
Book critic	132.288	Communications, Media
Interpreter	137.268	Communications, Media
Translator	137.288	Communications, Media
Publishing, graphic art	141.081	Communications, Media
Commercial designer	141.281	Communications, Media
Artist	144.081	Fine Arts, Humanities
Sculptor*	148.081	Fine Arts, Humanities
Music teacher	152.028	Fine Arts, Humanities
Musical composition	152.048	Fine Arts, Humanities
Announcer*	159.148	Communications, Media
Program director	159.168	Communications, Media
Accountant*	160.188	Business & Office

Job Title	D.O.T. Code	Cluster
Sales Manager*	163.118	Marketing, Distribution
Job analyst	166.088	Business & Office
Placement office	166.268	Business & Office
Office manager*	169.168	Business & Office
School board secretary	169.268	Public Service
Recreation supervisor*	187.118	Hospitality, Recreation
Theater manager	187.168	Business & Office
City manager	188.118	Business & Office
Air traffic controller	193.168	Transportation
Radio-telephone operator	193.282	Communications, Media
Urban planner	199.168	Construction
Secretary*	201.368	Business, Office
Court reporter	202.388	Business, Office
Telephone operator	203.138	Communications, Media
Typist*	203.588	Business, Office
File clerk	206.388	Business, Office
Clerk typist*	209.388	Business, Office
Bookkeeper*	210.388	Business, Office
Cashier	211.368	Business, Office
Desk clerk	211.468	Hospitality, Recreation
Computer operator	213.382	Business, Office
Keypunch operator	213.582	Business, Office
Data handler*	213.588	Hospitality, Recreation
Payroll clerk	215.488	Business, Office
Clerk*	219.388	Business, Office
Rate Clerk*	219.488	Transportation
Records clerk*	223.388	Environmental Control
PBX Operator*	235.862	Communications Media
Telephonist	236.588	Business, Office
Receptionist*	237.368	Hospitality, Recreation
Reservations clerk*	249.368	Hospitality, Recreation
Medical records clerk	249.388	Health
Broadcast checker	249.688	Communications, Media
Insurance agent*	250.258	Marketing, Distribution
Salesperson	289.458	Marketing, Distribution
Junk buyer	291.158	Marketing, Distribution
Newspaper route super.	292.138	Marketing, Distribution
Telephone surveyor*	293.358	Marketing, Distribution
Home lighting advisor	299.258	Environmental Control
Housewife	303.138	Consumer & Homemaking
Babysitter	307.878	Hospitality & Recreation
Barbering	330.371	Personal Service
Cosmetology	332.271	Personal Service
Wig dresser	332.381	Personal Service
Electrologist	339.371	Personal Service
Gateman	344.868	Personal Service
Ticket dispenser	349.780	Public Service
Orderly*	355.878	Health
Shoe repair	365.381	Personal Service
Fingerprint technician*	375.388	Public Service
Police dispatcher*	379.368	Communications, Media

Job Title	D.O.T. Code	Cluster
Vehicle driver	402.137	Transportation
Egg-washing machine operator	412.886	Agri-business, etc.
Dairy or milk tester	469.381	Agri-business, etc.
Plant supervision	529.132	Environmental Control
Dairy herd tester	529.886	Agri-business, etc.
Paint making	550.885	Fine Arts, Humanities
Tower operator	558.885	Marine Science
Metal pattern maker	600.280	Manufacturing
Tool & die maker	601.280	Manufacturing
Lapping machine operator	603.885	Manufacturing
Bench inspector	609.684	Manufacturing
Office machine assembly technician	633.281	Manufacturing
Lens edger	674.886	Manufacturing
Thread inspector	681.687	Manufacturing
Jewelry manufacturer	693.381	Manufacturing
Equipment maintenance	710.884	Manufacturing
Watch repair*	715.281	Manufacturing
Coil winder	724.281	Manufacturing
Electronics	726.281	Manufacturing
Electronics components inspector	726.687	Manufacturing
Motion picture projectionist	729.281	Communications, Media
Assembler small products	739.887	Manufacturing
Seamstress*	782.884	Manufacturing
Packer-sorter	784.887	Agri-business, etc.
Sewing machine operator	787.782	Manufacturing
Soldering machine operator	814.885	Manufacturing
Painter	840.781	Fine Arts, Humanities
Operations techniques	882.281	Marketing, Distribution
Airline dispatcher	912.168	Transportation
Taxi dispatcher*	919.168	Transportation
Ticket clerk	919.368	Transportation
Sign painter	970.381	Environmental Control
Assembly line worker	N.C.**	Manufacturing
Instrument repairs	N.C.	Personal Service
Dispatcher*	N.C.	Transportation
Artist*	N.C.	Fine Arts, Humanities
Musician	N.C.	Fine Arts, Humanities
IBM operator	N.C.	Business & Office
Teacher*	N.C.	Fine Arts, Humanities
Physician	N.C.	Health
Administrator*	N.C.	Public Service
Library worker*	N.C.	Hospitality, Recreation
Inventory efficiency analyst	N.C.	Marketing, Distribution
Technician*	N.C.	Health
Supervision	N.C.	Construction
Volunteer for elderly	N.C.	Public Service
Notary Public	N.C.	Public Service
Buyer	N.C.	Agri-business, etc.
Elected official	N.C.	Public Service
Clerical	N.C.	Business & Office
Machine operator	N.C.	Manufacturing

Job Title	D.O.T. Code	Cluster
Income tax consultant	N.C.	Personal Service
Lawyer	N.C.	Personal Service
Activity coordinator	N.C.	Hospitality, Recreation
Home mailing service	N.C.	Agri-business, etc.
Executive director	N.C.	Agri-business, etc.
Program director health agency	N.C.	Health
Editor & public relations	N.C.	Communications, Media
Mid-management	N.C.	Marketing, Distribution
Record information	N.C.	Business & Office
Health maintenance	N.C.	Health
Communications skills	N.C.	Construction
Processing techniques	N.C.	Construction
Management	N.C.	Marine Science
Purchasing	N.C.	Communications, Media
State Easter Seal Society	N.C.	Communications, Media
Div. of Public Relations Research	N.C.	Marketing, Distribution

Part B: In Wheelchair, Pushed by Someone

Job Title	D.O.T. Code	Cluster
Architect	001.081	Construction
Highway designer	005.081	Transportation
Statistician	020.188	Environmental Control
Marine science	041.081	Marine Science
School psychologist	045.108	Public Service
Market analyst*	050.088	Consumer & Homemaking
Speech therapist	079.108	Public Service
Dept. head, college	090.168	Fine Arts, Humanities
Teacher	091.299	Fine Arts, Humanities
Budget consultant	096.268	Construction
Script writer*	131.088	Communications, Media
Book critic*	132.288	Communications, Media
Translator	137.288	Communications, Media
Interpreter	137.268	Communications, Media
Sculptor	148.081	Fine Arts, Humanities
Announcer*	159.148	Communications, Media
Accountant*	160.188	Business & Office
Job analyst	166.088	Business & Office
Travel agent	168.268	Personal Service
School board secretary	169.268	Public Service
Vocational disability examiner	169.168	Business & Office
Radio operator	193.282	Communications, Media
Urban planner	199.168	Construction
Secretary	201.368	Business & Office
Typist	203.588	Business & Office
Clerk typist	209.388	Business & Office
Bookkeeper*	210.388	Business & Office
Desk clerk	211.468	Hospitality, Recreation
Computer operator	213.382	Business & Office
Keypunch operator	213.582	Business & Office
Clerk*	219.388	Business & Office

Job Title	D.O.T. Code	Cluster
Rate clerk	219.488	Transportation
Timekeeper*	223.388	Construction
PBX operator	235.862	Communications, Media
Receptionist*	237.368	Hospitality, Recreation
Reservations clerk*	249.388	Hospitality, Recreation
Medical records clerk	249.388	Health
Broadcast checker	249.688	Communications, Media
Insurance agent	250.258	Marketing, Distribution
Telephone surveys	293.358	Marketing, Distribution
Babysitting	307.878	Hospitality, Recreation
Barbering	330.371	Personal Service
Cosmetology	332.271	Personal Service
Orderly	355.878	Health
Shoe repair	365.381	Personal Service
Fingerprint technician	375.388	Public Service
Police dispatcher*	379.368	Communications, Media
Plant supervisor	529.132	Environmental Control
Watch repair	715.281	Personal Service
Assembler small products	739.887	Manufacturing
Seamstress	782.884	Manufacturing
Packer-sorter	784.887	Agri-business, etc.
Operations techniques	882.281	Marketing, Distribution
Taxi dispatcher*	919.168	Communications, Media
Ticket clerk	919.368	Transportation
Package handler	920.887	Marketing, Distribution
Sign painter	970.381	Environmental Control
Assembly-line worker	N.C.	Manufacturing
Instrument repairer	N.C.	Personal Service
Dispatcher	N.C.	Transportation
Artist	N.C.	Fine Arts, Humanities
Musician	N.C.	Fine Arts, Humanities
IBM operator	N.C.	Business & Office
Machine operator	N.C.	Manufacturing
Lab technician	N.C.	Health
Income tax consultant	N.C.	Personal Service
Lawyer	N.C.	Personal Service
Counselor*	N.C.	Public Service
Educator	N.C.	Public Service
Home mailing service	N.C.	Marketing, Distribution
Teacher*	N.C.	Fine Arts, Humanities
Administrator	N.C.	Public Service
Food technician	N.C.	Consumer, Homemaking
Library worker	N.C.	Hospitality, Recreation
Painter	N.C.	Hospitality, Recreation
Inventory efficiency analyst	N.C.	Marketing, Distribution
Equipment maintenance	N.C.	Health
Manager supplies	N.C.	Health
Dispatcher	N.C.	Transportation
Volunteer for elderly	N.C.	Public Service
Notary Public	N.C.	Public Service
Artist	N.C.	Fine Arts, Humanities

Job Title	D.O.T. Code	Cluster
Buyer	N.C.	Agri-business, etc.
Elected official	N.C.	Public Service
Clerical worker	N.C.	Business & Office
Executive	N.C.	Transportation
Menu planner	N.C.	Consumer, Homemaking
Auditor	N.C.	Business & Office
Record information	N.C.	Business & Office
Product inspector quality control	N.C.	Manufacturing
Health Maintenance	N.C.	Health
Processing techniques	N.C.	Construction
Management	N.C.	Marine Science
Estimator	N.C.	Construction

Part C: Leg Amputee

Job Title	D.O.T. Code	Cluster
Designer	002.081	Communications, Media
Radio engineer	003.187	Communications, Media
Mechanical engineer	007.081	Manufacturing
Landscape architect	019.081	Agri-business, etc.
Statistician	020.188	Agri-business, etc.
Research technician*	029.181	Environmental Control
School psychologist	045.108	Public Service
Researcher*	050.088	Marketing, Distribution
Medical technologist	078.381	Health
Speech therapist	079.108	Public Service
Occupational therapist	079.368	Health
Teacher*	091.299	Fine Arts, Humanities
Home economist*	096.128	Consumer & Homemaking
Consumer director of home economics	096.168	Consumer & Homemaking
Budget consultant	096.268	Construction
News analyst	131.068	Communications, Media
Script writer*	131.088	Communications, Media
Journalist*	132.268	Communications, Media
Book critic*	132.288	Communications, Media
Translator	137.288	Communications, Media
Commercial designer	141.281	Fine Arts, Humanities
Cameraman	143.062	Communications, Media
Artist	144.081	Fine Arts, Humanities
Sculptor	148.081	Fine Arts, Humanities
Music teacher	152.028	Fine Arts, Humanities
Broadcaster	159.148	Communications, Media
Accountant*	160.188	Business, Office
Manager supplies	162.158	Health
Public relations man	165.068	Business & Office
Job analyst	166.088	Business & Office
Placement office	166.268	Business & Office
Travel agent*	168.287	Personal Service
Vocational disability examiner	169.168	Business & Office

Job Title	D.O.T. Code	Cluster
School secretary	169.268	Public Service
Bank cashier	186.168	Business, Office
Custodian*	187.168	Personal Service
City manager	188.118	Business & Office
Assessor	188.188	Public Service
Air traffic controller	193.168	Construction
Radio operator*	193.282	Communications, Media
Case worker	195.108	Public Service
Urban planner	199.168	Construction
Radiation monitor	199.187	Consumer, Homemaking
Medical secretary*	201.368	Health
Court reporter*	202.388	Business & Office
Typist*	203.588	Business & Office
Record ward clerk	206.388	Health
Clerk typist	209.388	Business & Office
Bookkeeper*	210.388	Business & Office
Cashier	211.368	Business & Office
Toll collector*	211.468	Public Service
Computer operator	213.382	Business & Office
Keypunch operator	213.582	Business & Office
Payroll clerk	215.488	Business & Office
Marine scientist	219.388	Marine Science
Clerk*	219.388	Business & Office
Rate clerk	219.488	Transportation
Shipping clerk	222.138	Marketing, Distribution
Records clerk*	223.388	Environmental Control
Telephone answering service*	235.862	Communications, Media
Receptionist*	237.368	Hospitality, Recreation
Telephone surveyor	293.358	Marketing, Distribution
Reservations clerk*	249.368	Hospitality, Recreation
Watch repairer	249.387	Manufacturing
Medical records clerk	249.388	Health
Broadcast checker	249.688	Communications, Media
Insurance agent	250.258	Marketing, Distribution
Home service rep.	278.258	Consumer, Homemaking
Salesman	289.358	Marketing, Distribution
Salesperson	289.458	Marketing, Distribution
Junk buyer	291.158	Marketing, Distribution
Auctioneer	294.258	Marketing, Distribution
Home lighting advisor	299.258	Consumer & Homemaking
Bridal consultant	299.358	Marketing, Distribution
Housewife	303.138	Consumer & Homemaking
Cook	305.281	Personal Service
Babysitter	307.878	Hospitality, Recreation
Cocktail lounge hostess	310.868	Hospitality, Recreation
Bartender	312.878	Personal Service
Cook	315.381	Manufacturing
Checker	319.388	Marketing, Distribution
Barber*	330.371	Personal Service
Cosmetologist*	332.271	Personal Service
Wig dresser	332.381	Personal Service

Job Title	D.O.T. Code	Cluster
Electrologist	339.371	Personal Service
Gateman	344.868	Hospitality, Recreation
Ticket dispenser	349.780	Hospitality, Recreation
Motel recreation director	352.168	Hospitality, Recreation
Home attendant	354.878	Personal Service
Orderly	355.878	Health
Watchman	372.868	Construction
Fingerprint classifier	375.388	Public Service
Fish & game warden	379.168	Environmental Control
Police dispatcher	379.368	Communications, Media
Gardener	407.884	Agri-business, etc.
Egg-washing machine operator	412.886	Agri-business, etc.
Farmer	421.181	Agri-business, etc.
Artificial breeding tech.	467.384	Agri-business, etc.
Dairy or milk tester	469.381	Agri-business, etc.
Pyrometer man	512.687	Manufacturer
Dairy herd tester	529.886	Agri-business, etc.
Tower operator	558.885	Marine Science
Waste-treatment operator	559.782	Environmental Control
Metal pattern maker	600.280	Manufacturing
Machine operator	600.380	Construction
Lapping machine operator	603.885	Manufacturing
Drill press operator tape control	606.782	Manufacturing
Bench inspector	609.684	Manufacturing
Machine repairman	626.281	Manufacturing
Office machine assembly technician	633.281	Manufacturing
Printer*	652.885	Manufacturing
Cabinet maker	660.280	Construction
Lens edger	673.886	Manufacturing
Wire sawyer	677.782	Manufacturing
Thread inspector	681.687	Manufacturing
Jewelry manufacturer	693.381	Manufacturing
Equipment maintenance	710.884	Health
Watchmaker	715.281	Manufacturing
Coil winder	724.781	Manufacturing
Electronics technician	726.281	Manufacturing
Electronics component inspector	726.687	Manufacturing
Upholsterer	730.884	Personal Service
Seamstress	782.884	Manufacturing
Packer, sorter	784.807	Agri-business, etc.
Soldering machine operator	814.885	Manufacturing
Lather	842.781	Construction
Signalman	869.868	Construction
Septic tank serviceman	899.887	Construction
Tractor-trailer driver	904.883	Transportation
Truck driver	905.883	Transportation
Airline dispatcher	912.168	Transportation
Taxi driver*	913.363	Transportation
Ticket clerk	919.368	Hospitality, Recreation
Technical operator	930.188	Environmental Control
Service supervisor	954.782	Environmental Control

Job Title	D.O.T. Code	Cluster
Water filter cleaner	959.887	Environmental Control
Teacher*	N.C.	Hospitality, Recreation
Library worker	N.C.	Hospitality, Recreation
Painter	N.C.	Fine Arts, Humanities
Inventory efficiency analyst	N.C.	Fine Arts, Humanities
Technician	N.C.	Health
Supervisor	N.C.	Construction
Dispatcher*	N.C.	Transportation
Volunteer for elderly	N.C.	Public Service
Notary public	N.C.	Public Service
Legal services	N.C.	Public Service
Artist*	N.C.	Fine Arts, Humanities
Manager day care center	N.C.	Communications, Media
Buyer*	N.C.	Agri-business, etc.
Office manager	N.C.	Business & Office
Counselor*	N.C.	Personal Service
Inspector	N.C.	Construction
Lab Technician	N.C.	Marine Science
Asst. director YMCA	N.C.	Hospitality, Recreation
Clerical worker	N.C.	Business & Office
Repair services	N.C.	Public Service
Draftsman*	N.C.	Manufacturing
Office machine operator	N.C.	Manufacturing
Jewelry repairer	N.C.	Manufacturing
Editor & public relations	N.C.	Communications, Media
Publishing-graphic art	N.C.	Communications, Media
Menu planning	N.C.	Communications, Media
Radio dispatcher	N.C.	Communications, Media
Sales manager	N.C.	Marketing, Distribution
Estimator	N.C.	Construction
Salesperson	N.C.	Business & Office
Social worker	N.C.	Public Service
Politician	N.C.	Public Service
Vehicle driver	N.C.	Transportation
Workshop supervisor	N.C.	Public Service
Assembly line service	N.C.	Manufacturing
Driver	N.C.	Transportation
Musician	N.C.	Fine Arts, Humanities
IBM operator	N.C.	Business & Office
Machine operator	N.C.	Manufacturing
Lab technician*	N.C.	Health
Income tax consultant	N.C.	Personal Service
Lawyer	N.C.	Personal Service
Educator	N.C.	Public Service
Physician	N.C.	Health
Administrator	N.C.	Public Service
Activity coordinator	N.C.	Hospitality, Recreation
Home mailing service	N.C.	Marketing, Distribution
Mechanic	N.C.	Agri-business, etc.

Part D: Arm Amputee

Job Title	D.O.T. Code	Cluster
Radio engineer	003.187	Communications, Media
Biologist	041.081	Marine Science
Researcher	050.088	Marketing, Distribution
School psychologist	045.108	Public Service
Speech therapist	079.108	Public Service
Occupational therapy aide	079.368	Health
Home economist*	096.128	Consumer, Homemaking
Budget consultant	096.268	Construction
Script writer*	131.088	Communications, Media
Reporter	132.268	Communications, Media
Book critic*	132.288	Communications, Media
Interpreter	137.268	Communications, Media
Translator	137.288	Communications, Media
Commercial designer	141.281	Fine Arts, Humanities
Artist	144.081	Fine Arts, Humanities
Music teacher	152.028	Fine Arts, Humanities
Radio broadcaster*	159.148	Communications, Media
Program director	159.168	Communications, Media
Accountant*	160.188	Business & Office
Public relations man	165.068	Business & Office
Job analyst	166.088	Business & Office
Office manager	169.168	Business & Office
Custodian	187.168	Personal Service
Radio operator*	193.282	Communications, Media
Urban planner	199.168	Construction
Radiation monitor	199.187	Consumer, Homemaking
Secretary	201.368	Business & Office
Bookkeeper*	210.388	Business & Office
Data handler	213.588	Environmental Control
Payroll clerk	215.488	Business & Office
Timekeeper*	219.388	Construction
Records clerk	233.388	Business & Office
PBX operator*	235.862	Communications, Media
Receptionist*	237.368	Hospitality, Recreation
Reservations clerk*	249.368	Hospitality, Recreation
Broadcast checker	249.688	Communications, Media
Junk buyer*	291.158	Marketing, Distribution
Telephone surveyor	293.358	Marketing, Distribution
Home lighting advisor	299.258	Consumer & Homemaking
Housewife	303.138	Consumer & Homemaking
Yardman	304.887	Personal Service
Gateman	344.868	Hospitality, Recreation
Flagman	372.868	Construction
Forest service ad.	441.384	Agri-business, etc.
Dairy or milk tester	469.381	Agri-business, etc.
Pyrometer man	512.687	Manufacturing
Dairy herd tester	529.886	Agri-business, etc.

Job Title	D.O.T. Code	Cluster
Tower operator	558.885	Marine Science
Waste treatment operator	559.782	Environmental control
Machinist	600.280	Manufacturing
Bench inspector	609.684	Manufacturing
Cabinet maker	660.280	Manufacturing
Wire sawyer	677.782	Manufacturing
Thread inspector	681.697	Manufacturing
Electronics technician	726.281	Manufacturing
Fitter	801.281	Construction
Auto parts man	806.884	Transportation
Painter	840.884	Construction
Lather	842.781	Construction
Carpenter	860.381	Construction
Insulation hoseman	863.884	Construction
Roofer	866.381	Construction
Signalman	869.868	Construction
Septic tank serviceman	899.887	Construction
Taxi driver	913.363	Transportation
Taxi dispatcher	919.168	Communications, Media
Technical operator	930.188	Environmental Control
Service supervisor	954.782	Environmental Control
Water filter cleaner	959.887	Environmental Control
Food technician	N.C.	Consumer & Homemaking
Teacher*	N.C.	Hospitality, Recreation
Painter	N.C.	Fine Arts, Humanities
Manager supplies	N.C.	Health
Inventory efficiency analyst	N.C.	Marketing, Distribution
Mgr. day care center	N.C.	Communications, Media
Buyer*	N.C.	Agri-business, etc.
Counselor*	N.C.	Personal Service
Dispatcher*	N.C.	Transportation
Public elected official	N.C.	Public Service
Draftsman	N.C.	Manufacturing
Social worker*	N.C.	Public Service
Mid-management	N.C.	Environmental Control
Task analyst	N.C.	Hospitality, Recreation
Artist*	N.C.	Fine Arts, Humanities
Salesperson	N.C.	Business & Office
Politician	N.C.	Public Service
Easter Seal executive	N.C.	Public Service
Workshop supervisor	N.C.	Public Service
Driver	N.C.	Transportation
Income tax consultant	N.C.	Personal Service
Lawyer	N.C.	Personal Service
Educator	N.C.	Public Service
Market Manager	N.C.	Marketing, Distribution
Physician	N.C.	Health
Home worker	N.C.	Personal Service
Administrator	N.C.	Public Service

Part E: Poor Coordination

Job Title	D.O.T. Code	Cluster
Architect	001.081	Construction
Radio engineer	003.187	Communications, Media
Landscape architect	019.081	Agri-business, etc.
School psychologist	045.108	Public Service
Researcher	050.088	Marketing, Distribution
Speech therapist	079.108	Public Service
Budget consultant	096.268	Construction
Manager (radio, TV)	131.038	Communications, Media
News analyst, broadcaster	131.068	Communications, Media
Writer*	132.088	Fine Arts, Humanities
Copy writer	132.088	Fine Arts, Humanities
Book critic*	132.288	Communications, Media
Interpreter	137.268	Communications, Media
Translator	137.288	Communications, Media
Announcer*	159.148	Communications, Media
Program director	159.168	Communications, Media
Accountant*	160.188	Business, Office
Editor, public relations	165.068	Communications, Media
Job analyst	166.088	Business, Office
Travel agent	168.268	Personal Service
Vocational disability examiner	169.168	Business, Office
Recreation director	187.118	Hospitality, Recreation
Custodian*	187.168	Personal Service
Assessor	188.188	Public Service
Radio operator*	193.282	Communications, Media
Caseworker	195.108	Public Service
Urban planner	199.168	Construction
Secretary	201.368	Business & Office
Typist	203.588	Business & Office
File clerk	206.388	Business & Office
Bookkeeper*	210.388	Business & Office
Desk clerk	211.468	Hospitality, Recreation
Checker*	219.388	Marketing, Distribution
Stock broker	219.488	Business & Office
Telephone answering service	235.862	Communications, Media
Telephonist	236.588	Business & Office
Receptionist*	237.368	Hospitality, Recreation
Broadcast checker	246.688	Communications, Media
Reservations clerk*	249.368	Hospitality, Recreation
Junk buyer	291.158	Marketing, Distribution
Newspaper route sup.	292.138	Marketing, Distribution
Telephone surveyor*	293.358	Marketing, Distribution
Cook	313.381	Personal Service
Kitchen worker	318.887	Personal Service
Fingerprint classifier	375.388	Public Service
Police dispatcher	379.368	Communications, Media
Gardener	407.884	Agri-business, etc.
Upholsterer	780.884	Personal Service

Job Title	D.O.T. Code	Cluster
Signalman	869.868	Construction
Ticket clerk	919.368	Transportation
Stock boy	922.887	Marketing, Distribution
Teacher*	N.C.	Fine Arts, Humanities
Buyer	N.C.	Manufacturing
Counselor*	N.C.	Personal Service
Social worker	N.C.	Public Service
Administrator	N.C.	Public Service
Artist	N.C.	Fine Arts, Humanities
Income tax consultant	N.C.	Personal Service
Lawyer	N.C.	Personal Service
Educator	N.C.	Public Service
Post office employee	N.C.	Public Service
Lab technician	N.C.	Health
Rehabilitation counselor	N.C.	Health
Clerical worker	N.C.	Business & Office
Paramedical services	N.C.	Health

*Item reported by more than one respondent

**Note: N.C. = not codable—not possible to code item because of insufficient information.

Index